THE SECRET TO EVERYTHING

HOW TO LIVE MORE AND SUFFER LESS

NEEL BURTON

There is an old Japanese story about the Zen tea master Sen no Rikyu. One day, a Sakai tea man invited Rikyu to a tea ceremony in the hope of impressing him with an antique tea jar from China. But despite being served from the jar, Rikyu did not seem to notice it, commenting instead on the simple scenery outside the tea hut. When Rikyu left, the trader smashed the precious jar to pieces and withdrew in anger. Luckily, not all was lost. One of the other guests gathered the pieces and glued them together with golden lacquer. When he next came, Rikyu recognized the mended jar. 'Ah' he said, 'now it is magnificent!'

Created with Vellum

ABOUT THE AUTHOR

Dr Neel Burton is a psychiatrist, philosopher, and wine-lover who lives and teaches in Oxford, England. He is a Fellow of Green-Templeton College in the University of Oxford, and the recipient of the Society of Authors' Richard Asher Prize, the British Medical Association's Young Authors' Award, the Medical Journalists' Association Open Book Award, and a Best in the World Gourmand Award. His work has featured in the likes of Aeon, the Spectator, and the Times, and been translated into several languages.

www.neelburton.com

ALSO BY NEEL BURTON

The Meaning of Madness

Hide and Seek: The Psychology of Self-Deception

Heaven and Hell: The Psychology of the Emotions

For Better For Worse: Essays on Sex, Love, Marriage, and More

Hypersanity: Thinking Beyond Thinking

CONTENTS

INTRODUCTION

A few years back, I wrote a self-help book for people with low mood in which I argued that the journey out of depression is one of *learning*: learning about oneself, of course, but also learning life skills such as managing stress and coping with bad news, and, above all, learning to rediscover the little things that make life worth living and loving. I'm convinced that the experience of depression can open us out onto a richer and brighter future—whence the title of that book, *Growing from Depression*.

As the months rolled on and I heard back from readers and their relatives and carers, it became increasingly clear to me that everybody, and not just people with low mood, could benefit from this kind of learning and growing approach. After all, why wait until depression hits us to take action? If we start now, if we pre-empt it, maybe we can avoid depression altogether, and enjoy the benefits without also having to suffer the costs.

Separately, I also realized something else, namely, that there is a deep current running through all my work, in books like *Hide and Seek*, *Heaven and Hell*, and *Hypersanity*. On the surface, these books appear to be about a particular topic—respectively, self-deception, the emotions, and thinking skills—but underneath they all share a common theme and common thrust: how to live more and suffer less.

I began to look at my writing from this new 'self-help' perspective, more as a unified body than a collection of separate titles, and, as I did, I noticed something else...

Curiously, the same trope kept on resurfacing again and again all throughout my work, the same idea, but each time in a different context and a different form—almost as if, for all those years, I had been trying to tell myself something of the utmost importance.

These three insights began to dance together in the vestibule of my mind, until, one day, I thought: Well, why not write something more focused and practical, and build it around that central, recurring idea?

The title, *The Secret to Everything: How to Live More and Suffer Less*, immediately jumped out, with the 'secret' being none other than the idea itself, that startling truth that I had been trying for so long to tell myself.

This almighty secret is by no means original to me. It has been known to mystics and scholars for centuries and millennia, and, today, is increasingly being confirmed by both philosophy and science. Socrates certainly knew it, as did the Buddha, and more recently, Albert Einstein, Carl Jung, and Emily Dickinson. It is a secret not because it is hidden as such, but because it is so difficult to see, running counter to so many of our most basic assumptions.

This book leans on my other work but also includes a lot of new material. Each of the book's ten chapters exposes a particular aspect and practical application of the secret, while, at the same time, keeping the secret carefully under wraps. On the surface, the chapters may seem to have little in common, but they are all built around the same, universal wisdom.

Your challenge, as you read, is to unravel the secret, to find the common thread that runs through all the chapters.

The secret is discussed at the end, but don't peek or you'll spoil the fun.

I hope you enjoy the quest!

1

HOW TO SEE

> The hardest thing to see is what is in front of your eyes.
>
> — Friedrich Schiller

Gardening is more and more recognized, and now even prescribed by doctors, for its health benefits.

These include:

- Increased muscle strength and cardiovascular fitness.
- Improved sleep and diet (if you grow your own fruit and veg).
- Reduced stress, anxiety, and depression.
- A stronger sense of community and belonging, and
- Better self-esteem.

You don't even have to get your hands dirty: Some of these benefits accrue simply from visiting a garden, or even just looking over one—although it probably helps to notice and mentally engage with the greenery.

Researchers in South Korea randomly assigned patients recovering from thyroidectomy (surgery to remove the thyroid gland in the neck) to hospital rooms with plants and flowers, and hospital rooms without. They found that the patients in the rooms with plants and flowers fared significantly better, asking for less pain relief and requiring less time in hospital. So, yes, it makes sense to bring flowers, and, at home, to have indoor plants.

Even street trees greatly benefit our health. An American study looking at the city of Toronto found that, for cardio-metabolic conditions (heart disease, stroke, diabetes, obesity...), an increase of just 11 trees per city block could compare, in terms of health benefit, to an increase in annual personal income of $20,000.

How might gardening, and nature in general (including animals), help with mental health? To various degrees, we live inside the stories we tell ourselves. But gardening drags us out of our tortured heads and back into the natural world, which blunts the ideological and emotional extremes to which detached, abstract thought is prone.

In 1920, on the verge of a mental breakdown, the philosopher Ludwig Wittgenstein took up the post of assistant gardener at Klosterneuburg Abbey near Vienna, explaining in a letter to a friend that he had been longing for 'some kind of regularized work which, of all the things I can do in my present condition, is the most nearly bearable...'

Voltaire's *Candide* (1759) is an attack on the abstract and convoluted philosophy of Gottfried Wilhelm von Leibniz, and famously concludes with the precept, 'We must cultivate our garden.'

In the *Philosophy of Existence* (1938), Karl Jaspers described this disinterested process of looking outside oneself—or 'phenomenology', as it has been called—as 'a thinking that, in knowing, reminds me, awakens me, brings me to myself, transforms me'.

Just picture the gardener's pure and simple delight at the first crocuses or tulips, a bird's nest, a swarm of bees...

When we stop noticing small things, we are no longer truly alive.

Figure 1. The miracle of a robin on the garden fence.

The word 'phenomena' derives from the Ancient Greek meaning 'things that appear', and phenomenology can be defined as the direct examination and description of phenomena as they are consciously experienced.

Pioneered by Edmund Husserl (d. 1938) as a philosophical tool, phenomenology involves paying close attention to objects so that they begin to reveal themselves, not as we take them to be, but as they truly appear to naked human consciousness, shorn of superimposed theories and preconceptions. Pick out an object, plant, or animal, look at it, and then keep on looking for much longer than you normally would. Vision, said the painter James Ensor, changes as it observes.

As a method, phenomenology enables us to study not only the phenomena themselves, but also, by extension, the very structures of human experience and consciousness. This is not quite the same as mindfulness; and, unlike mindfulness, phenomenology has not yet seeped into popular consciousness.

The aim of mindfulness, which derives from Buddhist spiritual practice, is to increase our awareness and acceptance of incoming thoughts and feelings, and so the flexibility of our responses, which become less like unconscious reactions and more like conscious reflections. Phenomenology, in contrast, is more explicitly outward-looking—and, I think, much easier to practise.

Phenomenological activities such as gardening, writing, drawing, birdwatching, and wine tasting remove us from our stifled selves and return us to the world that we came from and were in danger of forgetting, reconnecting us with something much greater and higher than our personal problems and preoccupations. In that much, phenomenology can, quite literally, bring us back to life.

To describe is to know, to know is to understand, and to understand is to appreciate, enjoy, and even, to some extent, control. Like the more slippery mindfulness, phenomenology is a balm for depression, anxiety, and stress, and also boredom, loneliness, greed, selfishness, apathy, alienation, and any number of human ills.

If that were not enough, phenomenology also offers other kinds of benefit. I love gardening, but I also love ~~drinking~~ tasting wine

—and have even, somehow, written a book on wine and blind tasting.

Wine lovers often say that blind tasting (tasting a wine without knowing its identity) enables them to:

- Set a standard of objectivity.
- Test, stretch, and develop their senses.
- Apply their judgement.
- Recall old memories.
- Compare their analysis with that of their peers.
- Discuss the wine and learn about it, and about wine in general.
- Forge meaningful human relationships.
- Imbibe the wine with the respect and consideration that it deserves.

In refining their senses and æsthetic judgement, wine tasters become much more conscious of the richness not only of wine but also of other potentially complex beverages such as tea, coffee, and spirits, and by extension, the aromas and flavours in food, the scents in the air, and the play of light in the world.

For life is consciousness, and consciousness is life.

~

7 tips for being more in the moment

1. Start small and make it regular. For example, aim to go for a half-hour nature walk each day. Go no matter what, even if you're busy or it's raining. Having to go for a daily walk is one of the best things about owning a dog. People enjoy the disconnect of having to walk the dog because, actually, it's the dog that's walking them.

2. Make a change to your routine. Born in Königsberg in 1724, the philosopher Immanuel Kant was renowned for his strict routines. His neighbours could tell the time by his daily walks, and even nicknamed him 'the Clock of Königsberg'. He died in 1804, having in all his 79 years seldom left the city's precincts. When we are too set in our routine, we tend to take our surroundings for granted. This actually helped Kant, enabling him to live inside his head and become the abstract philosopher that he became. But for most of us, it can grow into a problem. By making small changes to our routine or surroundings, for example, going for an early morning walk, placing a pitcher of tulips on the kitchen table, we naturally notice things more. It's a bit like travelling, but on a smaller scale.

3. Simplify your life. When we are anxious or stressed, we tend to focus on our worries at the expense of the world around us. But the more we focus on our worries, the more stressed and anxious we become, setting up a vicious circle. We can break this vicious circle by cutting out certain things, even if that means doing less or doing only one thing at a time. At the very least, we need to make sure that we are getting adequate sleep and exercise, and that we are making the time, every so often, to do the things that we enjoy.

4. Practise deep breathing. In the shorter term, we can alleviate stress and anxiety (and even physical pain, as anyone who's been through childbirth knows) by regulating our breathing: Breathe in through your nose and hold the air in for several seconds. Then purse your lips and gradually let the air out, making sure that you exhale as far as you comfortably can. Continue doing this until you are feeling much more relaxed. Try it now, it'll only take a couple of minutes—and, I promise, you'll definitely feel the difference. Breath, said the Buddhist monk Thich Nhat Hanh, is the bridge which connects life to consciousness, which unites your body to your thoughts: 'Whenever your mind becomes scattered, use your breath as the means to take hold of your mind again.'

5. Cultivate idleness. There's a very fine divide between idleness and boredom. Most animals dislike boredom, but man, says the writer Colin Wilson, 'is tormented by it.' Boredom can open the shutters on some very uncomfortable thoughts and feelings, which we normally block out with a flurry of activity or with the opposite thoughts and feelings. We are, in the words of Virginia Woolf, 'always giving parties to cover the silence'. But idleness, and even boredom, can also have important upsides.

Here's one of my favourite Zen jokes:

> A Zen student went to a temple and asked how long it would take him to gain enlightenment if he joined the temple.
> "Ten years," said the Zen master.
> "Well, how about if I work really hard and double my effort?"
> "In that case, twenty years."

The more we rush, the less we contemplate; and the less we contemplate, the less we see and understand. Time is a very strange thing, and not at all linear: sometimes, the best way of using it is to 'waste' it.

6. Savour. Make an effort to enjoy whatever it is that you are doing. For example, when it comes to your main meal of the day, don't just lean on the kitchen counter and scoff it down lukewarm. Give it a bit of love and care, even if you're eating alone. Turn off the TV, set the table, dim the lights, and make a moment to feel grateful. Wine lovers don't just swallow their wine, they admire its hue, swirl it around in the glass, close their eyes and breathe it in deeply...

7. Focus on the process more than on the purpose, especially when it comes to repetitive, mundane tasks like cooking and gardening. When you paint a picture or write a book, it is there for ever (and isn't that just amazing?). But when you mow the lawn you have to do it all over again in just a few days' time. The gardener is like Sisyphus, the mythological king made to repeat for all eternity the same meaningless task of pushing a boulder up a mountain, only to see it roll back down again.

In his essay, *The Myth of Sisyphus* (1942), the philosopher Albert Camus concludes: 'The struggle to the top is itself enough to fill a man's heart. One must imagine Sisyphus happy.' Even in a state of utter hopelessness, Sisyphus can still be happy. Indeed, he is happy precisely because he is in a state of utter hopelessness, because in recognizing and accepting the hopelessness of his condition, he at the same time transcends it.

Notes

- F Schiller, *Ärzte*. 'The hardest thing to see is what is in front of your eyes.'
- Park SH & Mattson RH (2009): *Therapeutic influences of plants in hospital rooms on surgical recovery*. American Society for Horticultural Science, Online Feb 2009.
- Kardan O et al. (2015): *Neighborhood greenspace and health in a large urban center*. Scientific Reports 5:11610, Online 9 July 2015.
- L Wittgenstein and P Engelmann, *Letters from Ludwig Wittgenstein, with a Memoir* (New York: Horizon Press, 1974), p. 37.
- Voltaire (1759), *Candide*, XXX.

- K Jaspers (1939), *The Philosophy of Existence*, Introduction.
- Thich Nhat Hanh (1975), *The Miracle of Mindfulness.*
- V Woolf (1925), *Mrs Dalloway.*
- A Camus (1942), *The Myth of Sisyphus.*

2

HOW TO DREAM

Sleep is the best meditation.

— Dalai Lama

We spend about a third of our lives in sleep. But why do we sleep, and how can we do it better?

Sleep is critical to our cognitive performance and mental and physical health. Studies have found that sleep-deprived employees are less satisfied, less productive, and less creative. They are also more disinhibited, and more likely to engage in dishonest or unethical behaviour.

Cabin crew on long-haul flights suffer from frequent jet lag, which has been associated with cognitive deficits such as increased reaction times and impaired working memory. And despite being leaner and healthier than average, they are at a higher long-term risk of physical health problems such as cancer and diabetes.

According to the American Academy of Sleep Medicine (AASM), there are over 250,000 sleep-related motor vehicle accidents each year, and sleep-related accidents account for one in every five serious motor vehicle injuries. Strikingly, people who drive after 17 to 19 hours of wakefulness perform worse, on average, than people who are above the drink-drive limit.

Contrary to received wisdom, chronic sleep deprivation (a lack of sleep that builds up over time) is even more dangerous than total sleep deprivation (not sleeping at all). One study looking at cognitive deficits found that the long-term restriction of sleeping time to six hours or fewer could compare to up to two nights of total sleep deprivation. And unlike people with total sleep deprivation, people with chronic sleep deprivation are largely unaware of their deficits, and, so, more likely to endanger themselves and others.

Fatal insomnia, a rare prion disease of the brain, leads to confusion, delirium, and death within an average of just 18 months.

Adequate sleep, on the other hand, greatly improves learning and memory.

During sleep, the brain sorts out memories, consolidating useful or unusual ones and discarding unhelpful or 'duplicate' ones. Sleep also supports procedural memory, which is the memory of how to do things, such as chopping vegetables or riding a bicycle. Olympic athletes have come to recognize that sleep is just as important as diet and training, and aim to sleep at least eight hours a night, with many also making time for strategic daytime naps.

As well as memory, sleep enhances mood and cognitive function—one reason why we 'sleep on it' and 'sleep it off'. Experimental subjects who had their sleep restricted to four to five hours a night over one week reported feeling more stressed, angry, and sad. After returning to their regular routine, they experienced a dramatic improvement in mood. In people with a mental disorder such as depression or bipolar disorder, adequate sleep often suffices to prevent or forestall a relapse, and also plays a critical role in recovery.

In terms of physical health, the benefits of adequate sleep include fewer food cravings, greater weight loss, fewer viral infections, lower risk of cardiovascular accidents (strokes and heart attacks), lower risk of dementia, and longer life expectancy.

The cherry on the cake is that sleep also makes us look younger and more attractive, the so-called 'beauty sleep'.

To skimp on sleep is, clearly, a false economy.

Over the years, I think I've come to understand the secret to refreshing sleep.

During sleep, the brain cycles through four successive stages, the last of which is REM or 'rapid eye movement' sleep. Each four-stage cycle takes an average of about 90 minutes, with much more time spent in REM sleep towards the end of the night and just before natural awakening (Figure 2).

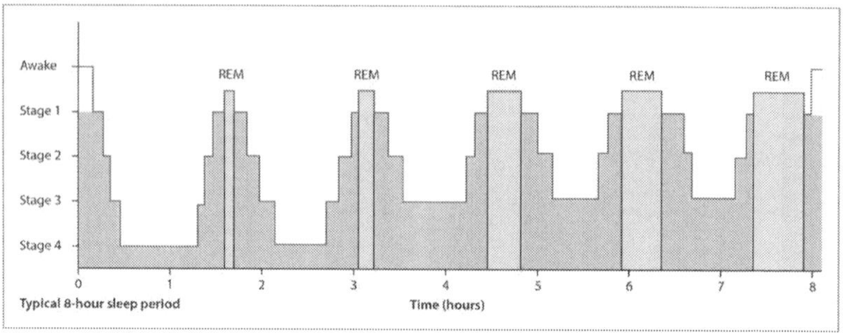

Figure 2. The sleep cycle over the course of one night. REM sleep builds up through the night.

Waking up after REM sleep is associated with feeling refreshed, and experimental subjects who were woken up after REM sleep performed better on tasks like anagrams and creative problem solving. In contrast, being woken up from deep non-REM sleep can leave us feeling groggy and grouchy—as though we had woken up 'on the wrong foot' or 'on the wrong side of the bed'.

REM sleep, as you know, is also associated with dreaming, which serves critical functions such as assimilating experiences, processing emotions, and generating and testing ideas. In fact, the brain can be more active during REM sleep than during wakefulness. Many great works of art have been inspired by dreams, including several of Edgar Allan Poe's poems and short stories, Salvador Dali's *Persistence of Memory*, and Paul McCartney's *Let It Be*.

The importance of REM sleep and dreaming to psychic health cannot be overstated. But because it is stacked towards the end of the night, a lot of this precious REM sleep can be sacrificed by sleeping short or waking up to an alarm clock or phone call —leaving us tired, confused, and irritable.

So, in a sentence, the secret to refreshing sleep is to wake up naturally after a sustained period of REM sleep.

Sleep is important on so many levels. Yet insomnia—difficulty falling or staying asleep—afflicts as many as one in three people, and almost everyone could do with better, more restorative sleep.

Short-term insomnia, which is the commonest type of insomnia, is often caused by a stressful life event, a poor sleeping environment, or an irregular routine. Other common causes of insomnia include poor sleeping habits ('sleep hygiene'), psychological disturbances such as anxiety and depression, physical problems such as pain and shortness of breath, prescription drugs, and alcohol and drug misuse.

Taking all these factors and more into account, here are my ten steps to happy sleep.

10 steps to happy sleep

1. Set up a fairly strict routine. Allocate a time for sleeping (for example, 11pm to 7am) and don't use this time for anything else. Avoid daytime naps or make them short and regular. If you have a bad night, avoid sleeping late, as this makes it more difficult to fall asleep the following night.

2. Wind down before bedtime. Devise a relaxing bedtime routine. This may involve breathing exercises or meditation, or simply reading a book or listening to some gentle music. A hot bath can be helpful: by diverting blood to the periphery, it leads, once out of the bath, to a fall in core body temperature, which in turn invites sleep. On the other hand, bright lights and bright screens can play havoc with your body clock, so avoid TV, computers, and phones around bedtime.

3. Eat a wholesome evening meal that contains a good balance of protein and carbohydrates. Eating too much can make it difficult to fall asleep; eating too little can disturb your sleep and decrease its quality. And don't leave it too late: dining late or eating just before bedtime can lead to indigestion or heartburn during the night.

4. Enjoy a hot, non-caffeinated drink before going to sleep. Good candidates include herbal tea, malted milk, and hot chocolate. But remember that sugar is a stimulant, so keep that to a minimum. In time, your hot drink could come to serve as a sleeping cue.

5. Avoid caffeine and alcohol, particularly in the evenings. Levels of adenosine in the brain rise with prolonged wakefulness, leading to sleepiness. Caffeine blocks adenosine receptors, which makes it harder to fall asleep and decreases the overall length and quality of sleep. Alcohol may make it easier to doze off, but, like caffeine, decreases the overall length and quality of sleep, and especially of restorative REM sleep.

6. Optimise your sleeping environment. Sleep in a familiar, dark, and quiet room that is adequately ventilated and neither too hot nor too cold. If possible, use this room for sleeping only, so that you come to associate it with sleep. In time, the room itself could serve as another sleeping cue. If necessary, wear a sleep mask and ear plugs. And switch off your phone. Small things can make a big difference: I find cool linen sheets very helpful at the height of summer, whereas in the depth of winter I like to have a thick, soft, cosy blanket on top of my regular bedclothes.

7. Don't get wound up. If sleep doesn't come, don't get anxious or annoyed and try to force yourself to sleep. The more aggravated you become, the less likely you are to fall asleep. Instead of tossing and turning, get out of bed and do something relaxing and enjoyable for half an hour before giving it another go.

I used to have a lot of trouble falling asleep. But now I can fall asleep almost at will, and I sleep very deeply. The key I think is to clear your mind and relax. You can try deep breathing (Chapter 1), or do what I do, which is to make myself feel grateful for the things we tend to take for granted, like being able to walk, or just being warm and safe in our bed. We'll come back to gratitude in the next chapter.

8. Shake your booty. Exercise (even just going for a walk) reduces arousal and anxiety and also helps with other aspects of psychological and physical health. For psychological health, it decreases stress, improves concentration and memory, boosts self-esteem, and directly lifts mood through the release of endorphins. For physical health, it slims down and tones the body, decreases blood pressure and heart rate, increases physical strength and endurance, and improves posture and flexibility. Physical activity is helpful in tiring us out, but it's also a short-term stimulant, so avoid exercising close to bedtime. In truth, any type of work, whether physical or mental, will tire us out—which is why having a 'lazy day' can make it much harder to fall asleep.

9. Reduce your overall stress. Apart from simplifying your life (Chapter 1), things that you can do to reduce stress include: going for a nature walk, giving and receiving massage, having a hot bath, laughing, singing, dancing, burning incense, and enjoying a delicious meal. Each of these activities should also give your endorphins a good boost. But beyond pleasure and relaxation, try to do something fulfilling each and every day, like working towards a long-term goal or making a (positive) difference to someone's life. As Leonardo da Vinci said, 'a well-spent day brings happy sleep'—and I would add, a well-spent life brings happy death.

10. If insomnia persists, speak to your doctor. In some cases, insomnia has a very specific cause, such as a physical problem or an adverse effect of medication, that requires your doctor's attention. While sleeping tablets may seem like a solution, they are best avoided in the longer term because of their adverse effects and high potential for tolerance (needing more and more to produce the same effects) and dependence—not to mention that the quality of drug-induced sleep may not be as high as that of natural, non-assisted sleep. Psychological alternatives to sleeping tablets that you can discuss with your doctor include cognitive behavioural therapy (CBT) and sleep restriction therapy.

Notes

- Christian MS & Ellis AP (2011): *Examining the effects of sleep deprivation on workplace deviance: A self-regulatory perspective*. AMJ 54(5):913-934.
- Naska A et al (2007): *Siesta in healthy adults and coronary mortality in the general population*. Arch Intern Med 167(3):296-301.
- American Academy of Sleep Medicine (2009). Drowsy Driving Fact Sheet (PDF).
- Williamson AM & Feyer AM (2000): *Moderate sleep deprivation produces impairments in cognitive and motor performance equivalent to legally prescribed levels of alcohol intoxication*. JOEM 57(10):649-55.

- Drummond SPA et al. (2006): *Effects of two nights sleep deprivation and two nights recovery sleep on response inhibition*. Journal of Sleep Research 15(3):261-5.
- Van Dongen HP et al. (2003): *The cumulative cost of additional wakefulness: dose-response effects on neurobehavioral functions and sleep physiology from chronic sleep restriction and total sleep deprivation*. Sleep 26(2):117-26.
- Rasch B & Born J (2013): *About sleep's role in memory*. Physiological Reviews 93(2):681-766.
- Dinges D et al. (1997): *Cumulative sleepiness, mood disturbance, and psychomotor vigilance decrements during a week of sleep restricted to 4-5 hours per night*. Sleep 20(4):267-277.

3

HOW TO BE RELIGIOUS

> I would maintain that thanks are the highest form of thought, and that gratitude is happiness doubled by wonder.
>
> — GK Chesterton

Both Western and Eastern religious traditions emphasize a number of related virtues such as gratitude, humility, and patience.

In many Christian denominations, the most important rite is the Holy Communion or Eucharist—a word which derives from *eucharistia*, Greek for 'thanksgiving'. Martin Luther himself spoke of gratitude as 'the basic Christian attitude'. Still today, many Christians express praise and gratitude several times a day in their prayers, as do, of course, Muslims and people of other faiths.

Gratitude never came easily to us men and women, and is a vanishing virtue in modern times. In our consumerist society, we tend to focus on what we lack, or on what other people have that we do not, whereas gratitude is the feeling of appreciation for all that we already have. More than that, it is the recognition that the good in our life can come from something that is beyond us and beyond our control—be it other people, nature, or a higher power—and that owes little or nothing to us.

Laughter is wise, because it broadens our perspectives, but gratitude is wiser still, because it broadens our perspectives beyond ourselves. In paying homage to something outside ourselves, gratitude enables us to connect with something that is not only larger than ourselves but also benevolent, even nurturing. By turning us outward, it opens our eyes to the miracle that is life, something to marvel at and revel in rather than ignore or take for granted as it passes us by.

Gratitude encourages us to joy, tranquillity, awareness, enthusiasm, and empathy, while removing us from anxiety, sadness, loneliness, regret, and envy, with which it is fundamentally incompatible. All this it does because it opens us out onto a bigger and better perspective, shifting our focus from what we lack or strive for to all that we already have, to the bounty that surrounds us, and, above all, to life itself, which is the fount of all opportunity and possibility. This eagle-eyed, god-like perspective frees us to live life, no longer for ourselves, but for life itself.

For this reason, the Roman philosopher Cicero called gratitude the greatest of the virtues, and, more than that, the mother of all the other virtues. But you don't have to take my or Cicero's word for it. Recent studies have linked gratitude with increased satisfaction, drive, and energy; reduced anxiety, stress, and sadness; and better sleep and overall physical health. Grateful people engage much more profoundly with their environment, leading to greater personal growth and self-acceptance, and stronger feelings of purpose, meaning, and connectedness.

In contrast, ingratitude—which can range from mere lack or absence of gratitude to Brutus' murder of Cæsar—is ignoble insofar as it ignores the contributions, efforts, and sacrifices of the benefactor, thereby affronting him or her, and, by extension, life itself. The irreligious philosopher David Hume inveighed that, 'of all the crimes that human creatures are capable of committing, the most horrid and unnatural is ingratitude...' For the philosopher Immanuel Kant, who we met in Chapter 1, ingratitude is, quite simply, 'the essence of vileness'.

Ingratitude, which, at least in the West, has become the norm, corrodes social bonds and undermines public trust, leading to societies built on rights and entitlements rather than duties and obligations, on 'me' rather than 'we', and in which every aspect of human life has to be regulated, recorded, and monitored.

~

Despite the great and many benefits that it confers, gratitude is hard to cultivate. It opposes itself to some deeply ingrained human traits, in particular, our need to feel in control of our destiny, our propensity to credit ourselves for our successes while blaming others for our shortcomings, and our unconscious belief in some kind of cosmic equality or justice that is being violated by the relative advantages of others. Today, we seek ever more to exist as independent agents rather than as a social collective, and gratitude undermines our sense of separateness, autonomy, and self-efficacy.

As human nature does not leave much place for it, gratitude is an attainment of maturity, or, to be more precise, emotional maturity, which can arrive at any age or, more commonly, not at all. Children who are taught to parrot 'thank you' mean it even less than their parents do. Even as adults, many people express gratitude, or a semblance of it, simply because doing so is useful or the 'done thing'. Gratitude is good manners, and good manners aim at aping profundity when profundity is lacking.

Genuine gratitude, on the other hand, is a rare and accomplished virtue. There is a fable in Æsop about a slave who extracts a thorn from the paw of a lion. Some years later, the slave and the lion are captured, and the slave is thrown to the lion. The starved lion bounds and roars towards the slave, but upon recognizing his friend fawns upon him and licks his face like a lapdog.

'Gratitude' concludes Æsop, 'is the sign of a noble soul'.

Like all virtues, gratitude requires constant cultivation, until such a day as we can say:

'Thank you for nothing!'

7 ways to be more grateful

1. Make more time for meditation or simple idleness. People who never stop tend to lose sight of the bigger picture. Finding time to stop and breathe and contemplate enables you to reframe things and regain perspective.

2. Practice shifting your focus from what you lack to all that you already have. Artists such as MC Escher teach us that what we regard as foreground and background is, to a large extent, a matter of choice and habit. See, for example, this striking lithograph.

3. Think back to some of the harder times in your life and compare them to your current situation. And ask yourself, 'In what ways have I changed compared to who I was then?'

4. Think of some of the people who are less fortunate than you are. Even better, volunteer to work or spend time with a few of these people.

5. Incorporate gratitude into your daily routine. For example, say a thankful phrase before your main meal of the day. Make this into a habit, even when you're eating alone. If anything, your food will taste better. And then, have grateful thoughts each night as your head hits the pillow. This should also help you to relax and fall asleep, and to sleep more soundly (Chapter 2).

6. Make a habit of thanking everyone for everything. When the time came for me to leave Japan (a virtually crime-free country), I arrived very early at the airport. When the check-in for my flight opened, precisely three hours before scheduled take-off, the staff lined up in front of their desks, pressed their hands together, closed their eyes, and bowed in unison at the gathering crowd of passengers—at which point I almost shed a tear. OK, I did. When I got back to England, having picked up the habit, I kept on nodding and bowing at everyone, which made me very popular while it lasted.

7. Remember to be grateful even for the small things, indeed, especially for the small things, the things that we tend to take for granted, like being warm and safe, or even just being alive in this world.

Notes

- GK Chesteron (1917), *A Short History of England*, Ch. 6. 'I would maintain that thanks are the highest form of thought, and that gratitude is happiness doubled by wonder.'

- Cicero, *Oratio pro Cn. Plancio*, 80.
- McCullough ME et al. (2002): *The grateful disposition: A conceptual and empirical topography*. Journal of Personality and Social Psychology 82:112-127.
- Wood AM et al. (2009): *Gratitude predicts psychological well-being above the Big Five facets*. Personality and Individual Differences 45:655-660.
- Wood AM et al. (2007): *Coping style as a psychological resource of grateful people*. Journal of Social and Clinical Psychology 26:1108-1125.
- D Hume (1738), *A Treatise of Human Nature*, III-I.
- I Kant, *Lectures on Ethics*. Cambridge University Press (2001).
- Æsop, *Fables*, The Slave and the Lion.

4

HOW TO BE WISE

> The mind is its own place, and in itself can make a heaven of hell, a hell of heaven.
>
> — JOHN MILTON

Every time I utter the word 'wisdom', someone giggles or sneers. Wisdom, more so even than expertise, does not sit comfortably in a democratic, anti-elitist society. In an age dominated by science and technology, by specialization and compartmentalization, it is too loose, too grand, and too mysterious a concept. With our heads in our smartphones and tablets, in our bills and bank statements, we simply do not have the time or mental space for it.

But things were not always thus.

The word 'wisdom' features 222 times in the Old Testament, which includes all of seven so-called 'wisdom books': Ecclesiastes, Job, Proverbs, Psalms, Sirach, the Song of Solomon, and the Book of Wisdom.

Here's a snippet from Ecclesiastes:

> For wisdom is a defence, and money is a defence: but the excellency of knowledge is, that wisdom giveth life to them that have it.

The word 'philosophy' [Greek, *philo* + *sophia*] literally means 'the love of wisdom', and wisdom is (or at least used to be) the overarching aim of philosophy.

In Plato's *Lysis*, Socrates warns the young Lysis that, without wisdom, he will be of no worth to anyone:

> If you are wise, all men will be your friends and kindred, for you will be useful and good; but if you are not wise, neither father, nor mother, nor kindred, nor anyone else, will be your friends.

The patron goddess of Athens, the city in which the *Lysis* is set, is none other than Athena, goddess of wisdom, who sprang out from the skull of Zeus clad in full armour.

Athena's symbol, and the symbol of wisdom, is the owl, a bird of prey which can cleave through darkness.

Indeed, the word 'wisdom' derives from the Proto-Indo-European root *weid-*, 'to see', and is related to a great number of modern English words including: advice, druid, evident, guide, Hades, history, idea, idol, idyll, view, Veda, vision, and visit.

In Norse mythology, the god Odin gouged out one of his eyes and offered it to Mimir in exchange for a drink from the well of wisdom, symbolically trading one mode of perception for another, higher one.

And the very name of our species, *Homo sapiens*, signifies 'wise man'.

But what exactly is wisdom?

People often speak of 'knowledge and wisdom' as though they might be closely related or even the same thing. So, one hypothesis is that wisdom is knowledge, or a great deal of knowledge.

But if wisdom is knowledge, then it has to be a certain kind of knowledge, or else learning the phonebook, or the names of all the rivers in the world, might count as wisdom.

And if wisdom is a certain kind of knowledge, then it is not scientific or technical knowledge, or else contemporary people would be wiser than even the wisest of ancient philosophers. Any twenty-first century school-leaver would be wiser than a Socrates or a Seneca.

Figure 3. Wiser than Socrates?

So let's look at a second hypothesis.

Once upon a time, Chærephon playfully asked the oracle at Delphi whether there was anyone wiser than his friend Socrates. To his surprise, the Pythian priestess replied that there was no one wiser.

To uncover the meaning of this divine utterance, Socrates questioned a number of people who laid claim to wisdom—politicians, generals, artists, and so on—and in each case concluded: 'I am likely to be wiser than he to this small extent, that I do not think I know what I do not know.'

Socrates was the wisest of all people not because he knew everything or anything, but because he knew what he did not know—or, more subtly, because he knew the limits of the little that he did know.

Still, there must be more to wisdom than mere 'negative knowledge', or else I could simply be super-skeptical about everything and count myself wise.

A third hypothesis is that wisdom consists in having very high epistemic standards, that is, in having a very high bar for believing something, and an even higher bar for calling that belief knowledge.

But then we are back to a picture of wisdom as something like scientific knowledge...

Confused? You ought to be.

Fortunately, Aristotle gives us a way out when he says, in the *Metaphysics*, that wisdom is the understanding of causes.

None of the senses (sight, hearing...) are regarded as wisdom because, although they can tell us a lot about the 'what', they cannot tell us very much about the 'why'.

Similarly, we suppose experts (scientists, artists...) to be wiser than mere technicians because experts understand distal causes, and can therefore teach, whereas technicians do not and cannot.

In other words, wisdom is not so much a kind of knowledge as a way of seeing, or ways of seeing. It is the understanding or appreciation of the right relations between things, which calls for more distant and removed perspectives, and maybe also the ability or willingness to shift between perspectives.

When we take a few steps back, like when we stand under the shower or go on holiday, or when we put ourselves into somebody else's shoes, we begin, if only for a time, to see the bigger picture.

In cultivating a broader perspective, it helps, of course, to be knowledgeable, but it also helps to be intelligent, reflective, open-minded, and disinterested—which is why we sometimes seek out and pay for 'independent' advice.

Above all, it helps to be brave, because the view from up there, though it can be exhilarating, and ultimately liberating, is at first terrifying—not least because it conflicts with so much of what we have been taught or programmed to think.

Courage, said Aristotle, is the first of the human qualities, because it is the one which guarantees all the others.

How to cope with bad news

Now let's put this idea of wisdom as perspective to the test and see how it might help us to cope with a sudden deterioration in our circumstances.

Imagine: Your partner cheated or walked out on you. You've been fired. Your house has been burgled. You've been diagnosed with a life-changing condition.

Bad news can leave us in a state of dread and despair. It seems like our whole world is falling apart, almost as if we're being driven into the ground. We fear the very worst and cannot get it out of our mind, or gut. Often, there are other emotions mangled in, like anger, guilt, despair, betrayal, and love.

Bad news: we've all had it, and the worst is yet to come.

So, how best to cope?

I'm going to give you three cognitive strategies that I picked up from the Stoic philosophers—who, in the second century, could count the Roman Emperor, Marcus Aurelius, among their ranks.

All three strategies aim, in one way or another, at generating perspective.

[While reading, hold a recent piece of bad news in the front of your mind, and consider how the strategies might or might not apply to your bad news.]

1. Contextualization

Try to frame the bad news, to put it into its proper context. Think about all the good things in your life, including those that have been and those that are yet to come. Remind yourself of all the strengths and resources—the friends, facilities, and faculties—that you can draw upon in your time of need. Imagine how things could be much, much worse—and how they actually are for some people. Your house may have been burgled. Yes, you lost some valuables and it's all such a huge hassle. But you still have your health, your job, your partner... Bad things are bound to hit us now and then, and it can only be a matter of time before they hit us again. In many cases, they are just the flip side of the good things that we enjoy. You got burgled, because you had a house and valuables. You lost a great relationship, because you had one in the first place. In that much, many a bad thing is no more than the removal or reversal of a good one.

2. Negative visualization

Now focus on the bad news itself. What's the worst that could happen, and is that really all that bad? Now that you've dealt with the worst, what's the best possible outcome? And what's the most likely outcome? Imagine that someone is threatening to sue you. The worst possible outcome is that you lose the case and suffer all the entailing cost, stress, and emotional and reputational hurt. Though it's unlikely, you might even do time in prison (it has happened to some, and a few, like Bertrand

Russell, did rather well out of it). But the most likely outcome is that you reach some sort of out-of-court settlement. And the best possible outcome is that you win the case, or better still, it gets dropped.

3. Transformation

Finally, try to transform your bad news into something positive, or into something that has positive aspects. Your bad news may represent a learning or strengthening experience, or act as a wake-up call, or force you to reassess your priorities. At the very least, it offers a window into the human condition and an opportunity to exercise dignity and self-control. Maybe you lost your job: time for a holiday and a promotion, or a career change, or the freedom and fulfilment of self-employment. Maybe your partner cheated on you. Even so, you feel sure that he or she still loves you, that there is still something there. Perhaps you can even bring yourself to understand his or her motives. Yes, of course it's painful, but it may also be an opportunity to forgive, to build a closer intimacy, to re-launch your relationship—or to go out and find a more fulfilling one. You've been diagnosed with a serious medical condition. Though it's terrible news, it's also the chance to get the treatment and support that you need, to take control, to fight back, to look at life and your relationships from another, richer perspective.

There's a Taoist story about an old farmer whose only horse ran away. 'Such terrible news!' said a neighbour. 'Maybe it is, maybe it isn't,' replied the farmer. The next day, the horse returned with six wild horses. 'Such wonderful news!' exclaimed the neighbour. 'Maybe it is, maybe it isn't,' replied the farmer. The day after that, the farmer's son tried to tame one of the wild horses but got thrown off and broke a leg. 'Such terrible news!'

cried the neighbour. 'Maybe it is, maybe it isn't,' replied the farmer, biting into a peach. A week later, war broke out: but thanks to his broken leg, the farmer's son managed to escape military conscription. 'It all worked out really well in the end,' said the neighbour, 'such great luck!'

'Maybe it is, maybe it isn't,' replied the farmer.

Notes

- John Milton, *Paradise Lost*, Bk. 1: 254-255. 'The mind is its own place, and in itself can make a heaven of hell, a hell of heaven.'
- Bible, OT, Ecclesiastes 7:12.
- Plato, *Lysis*. Trans. Benjamin Jowett.
- Plato, *Apology*.
- Aristotle, *Metaphysics*, Bk. Alpha.
- Aristotle, *Nicomachean Ethics*.

5

HOW TO BE FEARLESS

Anxiety is the dizziness of freedom.

— Søren Kierkegaard

In my textbook of psychiatry, I define anxiety as 'a state consisting of psychological and physical symptoms brought about by a sense of apprehension at a perceived threat'. Fear is similar to anxiety except that with fear the threat is, or is perceived to be, more concrete, present, or imminent.

Fear and anxiety can, of course, be a normal response to life experiences, sophisticated protective mechanisms that have evolved to prevent us from entering into potentially dangerous situations, and to help us escape from them should they befall us regardless.

For example, anxiety can prevent us from coming into close contact with disease-carrying or venomous animals such as rats, snakes, and spiders; from engaging with a much stronger or angrier enemy; and even from declaring our undying love to someone who is unlikely to spare our feelings.

If we do, nonetheless, find ourselves caught up in a potentially dangerous situation, the release of adrenaline triggered by fear can help us to mount an appropriate response by priming our body for action and increasing our performance and stamina.

In short, the purpose of fear and anxiety is to protect us from harm and, above all, to preserve us from death—whether literal or figurative, biological or psychosocial.

~

On the other hand, severe or inappropriate anxiety can be maladaptive, preventing us from doing the sorts of things that most people take for granted such as leaving the house or even our bedroom. I once treated a patient with a severe anxiety disorder who, to avoid crossing the corridor from bed to toilet, urinated into a bottle and defæcated into a plastic bag.

Such pathological anxiety is increasingly common in our society, and often presents in one or more distinct patterns or syndromes such as phobia, panic disorder, or post-traumatic stress disorder (PTSD). These pathological forms of anxiety, like the adaptive forms, can readily be interpreted in terms of life and death. Let's look at each one in turn.

The commonest phobias such as arachnophobia (spiders), ophidiophobia (snakes), acrophobia (heights), achluophobia (darkness), and brontophobia (storms) are all for the sorts of dangers that commonly threatened our ancestors. Today, modern, man-made hazards such as motor cars and electric cables are much more likely to strike us down, yet most phobias remain for natural dangers, presumably because technological hazards are too recent to have imprinted themselves onto our genome.

Panic disorder involves recurrent panic attacks during which symptoms of anxiety are so severe that the person fears that she is suffocating, having a heart attack, or losing control. Very soon, the person develops a fear of the panic attacks themselves, which in turn sets off further panic attacks. A vicious circle takes hold, with the panic attacks becoming ever more frequent and severe and even occurring 'out of the blue'.

As with phobias, the ulterior fear in panic disorder is of death and dying, as it is also in PTSD, which is a reaction to a traumatic life event such as a car crash or physical or sexual assault. Common symptoms of PTSD include anxiety, of course, but also numbing, detachment, flashbacks, nightmares, and loss of memory for the traumatic event.

The symptoms of PTSD vary significantly from one culture to another, so much so that PTSD is sometimes thought of as a 'culture-bound syndrome'. Culture-bound syndromes are essentially culture-specific anxiety disorders, which, again, like all anxiety disorders, can easily be understood in terms of life and death.

Dhat, for example, seen in South Asian men, involves sudden fear about loss of semen in the urine, whitish discolouration of the urine, and sexual dysfunction, accompanied by feelings of weakness and exhaustion. Dhat may be rooted in the old Hindu belief that it takes forty drops of blood to create a drop of bone marrow, and forty drops of bone marrow to create a drop of semen, and thus that semen is a concentrated essence of life.

In addition to fear and anxiety and their various pathological forms (such as phobias, panic disorder, etc.), there is a more abstract form of anxiety that has been dubbed 'existential anxiety'.

What is existential anxiety?

In his influential paper of 1943, *A Theory of Human Motivation*, the psychologist Abraham Maslow proposed that healthy human beings have a certain number of needs, and that these needs can be arranged in a hierarchy, with some needs (such as physiological and safety needs) being more primitive or basic than others (such as social and ego needs).

Maslow's so-called 'hierarchy of needs' is often presented as a five-level pyramid (Figure 4), with higher needs coming into focus only once lower, more basic needs have been met.

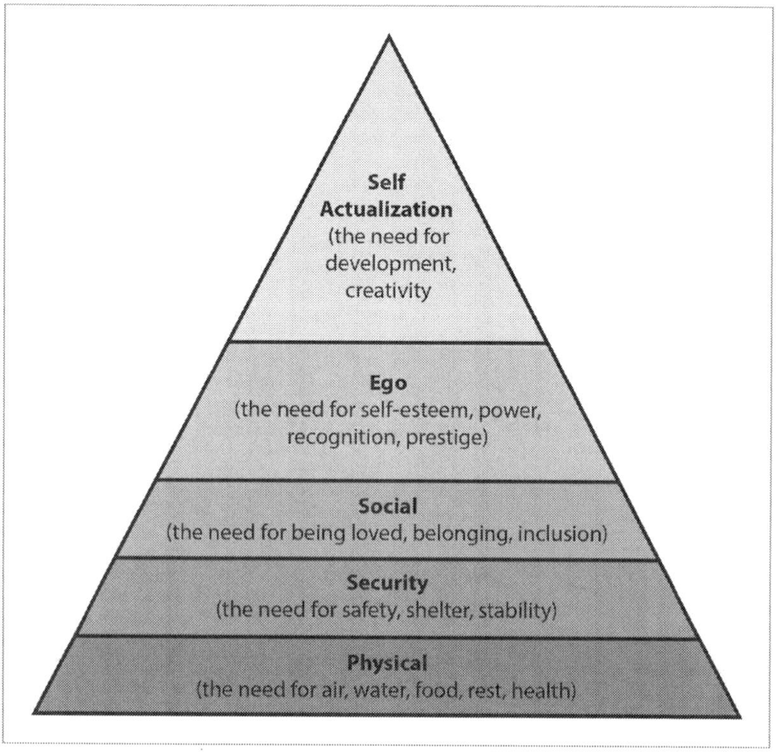

Figure 4. Maslow's hierarchy of needs.

Maslow called the bottom four levels of the pyramid 'deficiency needs' because we do not feel anything if they are met but become anxious or distressed if they are not. Thus, physiological needs such as eating, drinking, and sleeping are deficiency needs, as are safety needs, social needs such as friendship and sexual intimacy, and ego needs such as self-esteem and recognition.

On the other hand, he called the fifth, top level of the pyramid a 'growth need' because our need to self-actualize obliges us to go beyond our individual, limited selves and fulfil our full potential as human beings.

Once we have met our deficiency needs, the focus of our anxiety shifts to self-actualization, and we begin, even if only at a sub- or semi-conscious level, to contemplate our bigger picture. However, only a small minority of people are able to self-actualize because self-actualization calls upon uncommon qualities such as independence, awareness, creativity, originality, and, of course, courage.

Maslow's hierarchy of needs has been criticized for being overly schematic, but it presents an intuitive and potentially useful theory of human motivation. After all, there is truth in the saying that one cannot philosophize on an empty stomach.

Many people who have met all their deficiency needs remain unable to self-actualize, instead inventing more deficiency needs for themselves, because to contemplate the meaning of life would lead them to entertain the possibility of its meaninglessness and the prospect of their own death and annihilation.

A person who begins to contemplate her bigger picture may come to fear that life is meaningless and death inevitable, but at the same time cling on to the cherished belief that her life is eternal or important or at least significant. This gives rise to an inner conflict, and the inner conflict to existential anxiety.

While fear and anxiety and their pathological forms (such as phobias, panic disorder, etc.) are grounded in threats to life, existential anxiety is rooted in the brevity and apparent absurdity or meaninglessness of life.

Existential anxiety is so disturbing that most people avoid it at all costs, constructing a false reality out of goals, aspirations, habits, customs, values, culture, and religion in a bid to deceive themselves that their lives are special and meaningful, and that death is distant or delusory.

Unfortunately, such self-deception comes at a heavy price. According to the philosopher Jean-Paul Sartre, people who refuse to face up to 'non-being' are acting in 'bad faith' and living out a life that is inauthentic, that is constrained, contrived, and unfulfilling.

Facing up to non-being can bring insecurity, loneliness, responsibility, and consequently anxiety, but it can also bring a sense of calm, freedom, and even nobility. Far from being pathological, existential anxiety is a necessary transitional phase, a sign of health, strength, and courage, and a harbinger of bigger and better things to come.

For the Harvard philosopher and theologian Paul Tillich, refusing to face up to non-being leads not only to inauthenticity, as per Sartre, but also to pathological (or 'neurotic') anxiety.

In *The Courage to Be* (1952), Tillich wrote:

> He who does not succeed in taking his anxiety courageously upon himself can succeed in avoiding the extreme situation of despair by escaping into neurosis. He still affirms himself but on a limited scale. Neurosis is the way of avoiding nonbeing by avoiding being.

According to this striking outlook, pathological anxiety, although seemingly grounded in threats to life, in fact arises from repressed existential anxiety, which itself arises from our uniquely human capacity for self-consciousness.

Facing up to non-being enables us to put our life into perspective, see it in its entirety, and thereby lend it a sense of direction and unity. If the ultimate source of anxiety is fear of the future, the future only ends in death; and if the ultimate source of anxiety is uncertainty, death is the only certainty.

It is only by facing up to death, accepting its inevitability, and integrating it into a life that we can escape from the pettiness and paralysis of anxiety, and, in so doing, free ourselves to make, and get, the most out of our lives.

This esoteric understanding is what I have come to call 'the philosophical cure for fear and anxiety'.

How to eliminate anxiety by facing up to death

The ancient philosopher Epicurus of Samos, who flourished not long after Aristotle died, founded a school of philosophy that convened at his home and garden in Athens.

Called 'the Garden', this school dedicated itself to attaining happiness through the exercise of reason and rational principles, and, in a highly stratified and sexist society, admitted both women and slaves.

According to Epicurus, reason, if we follow it, teaches that pleasure is good and pain bad, and that pleasure and pain are the ultimate measures of good and bad.

This has often been misconstrued as a call for rampant hedonism, rather than the absence of pain and tranquillity of mind ('ataraxia') that Epicurus actually intended. In fact, Epicurus explicitly warned against overindulgence, since overindulgence so often leads to pain.

Epicurus wrote prolifically but, unfortunately, the early Christians thought of him as especially profane among the pagan philosophers, and almost none of his works survived their opprobrium.

Epicurus held that the gods exist but have no care or concern for humankind. Indeed, for them to involve themselves in the menial matters of men would be to perturb the supreme happiness and tranquillity that characterizes and defines them.

So, instead of fearing the gods, we would do better to emulate them in their serenity and detachment.

Along with the fear of the gods, the other major obstacle to ataraxia is the fear of death. But this fear is misplaced, and this for two main reasons:

1. The mind is a part of the body, and, just like other parts of the body (and everything else in the universe), is made up of atoms. The death of a person entails the death of both body and mind and the re-dispersion of their atoms. As there is no longer any person to be troubled, death cannot trouble the person after she is dead. And if death cannot trouble the person after she

is dead, then nor should it trouble her while she is still alive.

2. The eternity that comes before a person's birth is not regarded as an evil, and, so, nor should the eternity that comes after her death.

These two arguments are early formulations of, respectively, the 'no subject of harm argument' and the 'symmetry argument', which have, among professional philosophers, more or less withstood the test of time.

Epicurus himself died at the age of 72 from renal colic (kidney stones), which is associated with one of the sharpest and most intense of all bodily pains.

On the last day of his life, he penned this remarkable letter, a testament to the overriding powers of philosophy, to his friend and follower Idomeneus:

> I have written this letter to you on a happy day to me, which is also the last day of my life. For I have been attacked by a painful inability to urinate, and also dysentery, so violent that nothing can be added to the violence of my sufferings. But the cheerfulness of my mind, which comes from the recollection of all my philosophical contemplation, counterbalances all these afflictions. And I beg you to take care of the children of Metrodorus, in a manner worthy of the devotion shown by the young man to me, and to philosophy.

Death not only deprives us of life, but also compels us to spend the life that it deprives us from in the mostly unconscious fear of this deprivation.

We cannot cheat death, or not for very long. But what we can do is come to terms with death in the hope of preventing it from preventing us from making the most of our lives.

Notes

- S Kierkegaard (1844), *The Concept of Anxiety*.
- A Maslow (1943), *A Theory of Human Motivation*.
- JP Sartre (1946), *Existentialism Is a Humanism*.
- P Tillich (1952), *The Courage to Be*.
- Diogenes Lærtius, *Lives and Opinions of Eminent Philosophers*, Bk. 10, Epicurus.

6

HOW TO LIVE

> Those who have a 'why' to live, can bear with almost any 'how'.
>
> — Viktor Frankl

The question of the meaning of life is perhaps one that we would rather not ask, for fear of the answer or lack thereof.

Still today, many people believe that we, humankind, are the creation of a supernatural entity called God, that God had an intelligent purpose in creating us, and that this intelligent purpose is 'the meaning of life'.

I do not propose to rehearse the various arguments for and against the existence of God, and still less to take a side. But even if God exists, and even if He had an intelligent purpose in creating us, no one really knows what this purpose might be, or that it is especially meaningful.

The Second Law of Thermodynamics states that the entropy of a closed system such as the universe increases up to the point at which an equilibrium is reached, and God's purpose in creating us, and, indeed, all of nature, might have been no more lofty or uplifting than to catalyse this process in the same manner that soil organisms catalyse the decomposition of organic matter.

If our God-given purpose is to serve as super-efficient heat dissipators, then having no purpose at all is better than having this sort of purpose—because it frees us to be the authors of our own purpose or purposes, and so to lead truly dignified and meaningful lives.

In that much, having no purpose at all is better than having any kind of pre-determined purpose, even more traditional, uplifting ones such as serving God, testing our mettle, or improving our karma.

In short, even if God exists, and even if He had an intelligent purpose in creating us (and why should He have had?), we do not know what this purpose might be, and, whatever it might be, we would rather be able to do without it, or at least to ignore or discount it.

For unless we can be free to become the authors of our own purpose or purposes, our lives may have, at worst, no purpose at all, and, at best, only some unfathomable and potentially trivial purpose that is not of our own choosing.

You may object, like many people do, that not to have a pre-determined purpose is, really, not to have any purpose at all.

But this is to believe that for something to have a purpose, it must have been created with a particular purpose in mind, and, moreover, must still be serving that original purpose.

Some years ago, I visited the vineyards of Châteauneuf-du-Pape in the South of France. One evening, I picked up a rounded stone called a *galet* which I took back to Oxford and put to good use as a book-end.

In the vineyards of Châteauneuf-du-Pape, these stones serve to capture the heat of the sun and release it back into the cool of the night, helping the thick-skinned grapes to ripen.

Of course, these stones were not created with this or any other purpose in mind. Even if they had been created for a purpose, it would almost certainly not have been to make great wine or serve as book-ends.

That same evening over supper, I got my friends to blind taste a bottle of Bordeaux wine. To disguise the bottle, I slipped it into one of a pair of socks. Unlike the galet, the sock had been created with a definite purpose in mind, albeit one very different from (although not strictly incompatible with) the one that it came to assume on that joyful evening.

You might yet object that talk about the meaning of life is neither here nor there because life is merely a prelude to some form of eternal afterlife and this, if you will, is its purpose.

But I can marshal up at least three arguments against this position:

1. It is not at all clear that there is, or even can be, some form of eternal afterlife that entails the survival of the personal ego.
2. Even if there could be and were such an afterlife, living for ever is not in itself a purpose. The concept of the

afterlife merely displaces the problem to one remove, begging the question: what then is the purpose of the afterlife? If the afterlife has a pre-determined purpose, again, we do not know what that is, and, whatever it is, we would rather be able to do without it.

3. Reliance on an eternal afterlife not only postpones the question of life's purpose, but also dissuades us from determining a purpose or purposes for what may be the only life that we do have.

So, whether or not God exists, whether or not He gave us a purpose, and whether or not there is an eternal afterlife, we are better off creating our own purpose or purposes.

To put it in Sartrean (or existentialist) terms, whereas for the *galet* it is true only that existence precedes essence, for the sock it is true both that essence precedes existence (when the sock is used on a human foot) *and* that existence precedes essence (when the sock is used for an originally unintended purpose, for example, as a bottle sleeve).

We human beings are either like the rock or the sock, but whichever we are like, we are better off creating our own purpose or purposes.

Plato once defined man as an animal, biped, featherless, and with broad nails (thereby excluding plucked chickens); but another, much better definition that he gave was simply this: 'A being in search of meaning.'

Human life may not have been created with any pre-determined purpose, but this need not imply that it cannot have a purpose, or that this purpose cannot be just as good as, if not much better than, any pre-determined one.

And so the meaning of life, of our life, is that which we choose to give it.

But how to choose?

How to give our life a meaning

In *Man's Search for Meaning*, the psychiatrist and neurologist Viktor Frankl wrote about his ordeal as a concentration camp inmate during the Second World War.

Interestingly, Frankl found that those who survived longest in the concentration camp were not those who were physically strong, but those who retained a sense of control over their environment.

He observed:

> We who lived in concentration camps can remember the men who walked through the huts comforting others, giving away their last piece of bread. They may have been few in number, but they offer sufficient proof that everything can be taken from a man but one thing: the last of human freedoms—to choose one's own attitude in any given set of circumstances—to choose one's own way.

Frankl's message is ultimately one of hope: even in the most absurd, painful, and dispiriting of circumstances, life can still be given a meaning, and so too can suffering.

Life in the concentration camp taught Frankl that our main drive or motivation in life is neither pleasure, as Freud had believed, nor power, as Adler had, but *meaning*.

After his release, Frankl founded the school of logotherapy [Greek, *logos*, 'word', 'reason', or 'principle'], which is sometimes referred to as the 'Third Viennese School of Psychotherapy' for coming after those of Freud and Adler.

The overarching aim of logotherapy is to carry out an existential analysis of the person, and, in so doing, help her uncover or discover meaning for her life.

According to Frankl, meaning can be found through:

- Experiencing reality by interacting authentically with the environment and with others.
- Giving something back to the world through creativity or self-expression, and,
- Changing our attitude when faced with a situation or circumstance that we are unable to change.

'The point', said Frankl, 'is not what we expect from life, but rather what life expects from us.'

Notes

- V Frankl (1946), *Man's Search for Meaning*. 'Those who have a 'why' to live, can bear with almost any 'how'.'
- JP Sartre (1946), *Existentialism Is a Humanism*.

7

HOW TO LOVE

> He whom love touches not walks in darkness.
>
> — Plato

Once upon a time, people used to find meaning in God.

But over the centuries, the sacred seeped out of God and into romantic love, which came to take the place of the waning religion in lending purpose to our lives.

People had once loved God, but now they loved love: more than with their beloved, they fell in love with love itself.

Today, we all seem to be hankering after romantic love. But few of us realize that, far from being timeless and universal, romantic love is a modern construct that emerged in tandem with the novel.

In *Madame Bovary* (1856), itself a novel, Gustave Flaubert tells us that Emma Bovary only found out about romantic love through 'the refuse of old lending libraries'.

These books, he wrote,

> ...were all about love and lovers, damsels in distress swooning in lonely lodges, postillions slaughtered all along the road, horses ridden to death on every page, gloomy forests, troubles of the heart, vows, sobs, tears, kisses, rowing-boats in the moonlight, nightingales in the grove, gentlemen brave as lions and gentle as lambs, too virtuous to be true, invariably well-dressed, and weeping like fountains.

In ancient times, people did of course fall in love, but they did not believe that their love might in some sense save them, as we tend to today.

When, in Homer's *Iliad*, Helen eloped with Paris, neither she nor he conceived of their attraction as pure or noble or exalting.

If you think about it, the concept of romantic love barely features among the 66 books of the Bible.

In the Bible, all love is directed at God, and the love for the spouse and more generally for the other is subsumed under the love of God.

In the Binding of Isaac, Abraham's love for God trumps his love for Isaac his longed-for son, whom he is willing to sacrifice for no other reason than that God commanded it.

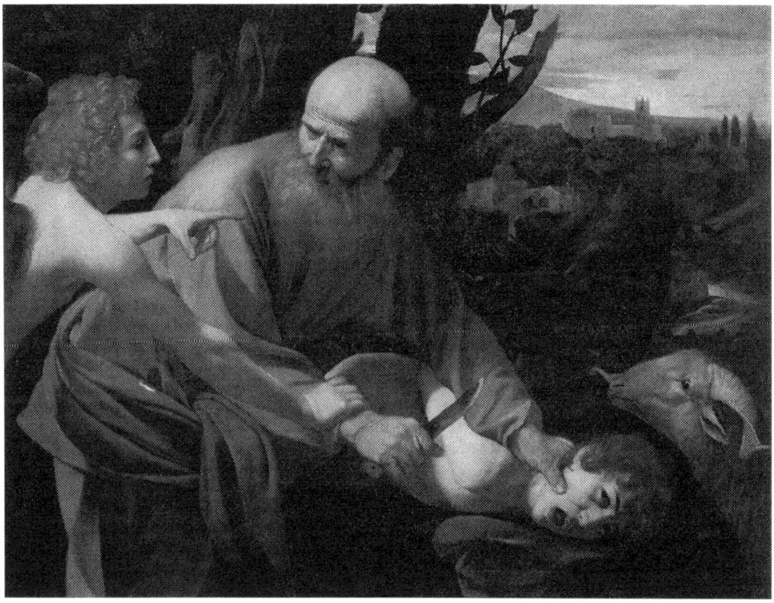

Figure 5. The Sacrifice of Isaac, by Caravaggio (c. 1603). The Uffizi Galleries, Florence.

The two greatest love stories in the Bible are not of husband and wife, nor even of man and woman, but of man and man, and woman and woman.

Upon learning of Jonathan's death on Mount Gilboa, David laments: 'I am distressed for thee, my brother Jonathan: very pleasant hast thou been unto me: thy love to me was wonderful, passing the love of women.'

In the Book of Ruth, a famine leads Naomi, Elimelech, and their two sons to move from Bethlehem to Moab. In time, Elimelech dies, as do their two sons, leaving Naomi and her two daughters-in-law destitute.

Naomi decides to return to Bethlehem, entreating her daughters-in-law, who are Moabites and thus from a different ethnic group, not to follow in her barren footsteps.

But one daughter-in-law, Ruth, insists upon accompanying her in the strongest possible terms:

> Intreat me not to leave thee, or return from the following after thee: for whither thou goest, I will go; and where thou lodgest, I will lodge: thy people shall be my people, and thy God my God: Where thou diest, I will die, and there will be buried...

I don't know about you, but that sounds more like a marriage vow than anything I might say to my mother-in-law.

Abraham had surrendered himself and Isaac out of love for God. But in the Romantic era, love became all the opposite: a means of finding and validating oneself, of lending weight and texture to one's life—as encapsulated by Sylvester's 1978 hit, *You Make Me Feel (Mighty Real)*, the final kissing scene in *Cinema Paradiso*, and countless other popular songs and films.

In the time of God, 'finding oneself'—or, more accurately, losing oneself in God—had demanded years of patient spiritual practice. But after the French Revolution, romantic love could come to the rescue of the first pair of buffoons, with very little effort or sacrifice required on either one's part. Being saved became simply a matter of luck.

But there are, of course, a number of problems with the notion of romantic love.

We might not find it, and, if we do, it might not be reciprocated. Even if we do find it and it is reciprocated, it is largely manufactured, arising from our own needs and notions rather than any real properties or qualities of the beloved. And, so, even if it lasts, romantic love is likely to lead to disillusionment and, with that, to pain.

More important still, by preoccupying ourselves with romantic love, we risk neglecting other types of love that are more stable or readily available, and that may, especially in the longer term, prove more healing and fulfilling.

The 7 types of love

The Ancient Greeks had several words for love, enabling them to distinguish more clearly between the different types.

I'm now going to guide you through seven types of love, each with a name from Ancient Greek. These seven types of love are loosely based on classical readings, especially of Plato and Aristotle, and on JA Lee's 1973 book, *Colors of Love*.

1. Eros

Eros is sexual or passionate love, and most akin to the modern construct of romantic love.

In Greek myth, it is a form of madness brought about by one of Cupid's arrows. The arrow breaches us and we 'fall' in love, as did Paris with Helen, leading to the downfall of Troy and much of the federated Greek army.

In the *Antigone* of Sophocles, the chorus sings: 'Love... whoever feels your grip is driven mad... you wrench the minds of the righteous into outrage, swerve them to their ruin...'

In modern times, eros has been amalgamated with the broader life force, something akin to Schopenhauer's will, a blind process of striving for survival and reproduction that runs through all of nature.

Eros has also been contrasted with *Logos*, or Reason, and Cupid painted as a blindfolded child.

2. Philia

The hallmark of *philia*, or friendship, is shared goodwill.

Aristotle taught that a person can bear goodwill to another for one of three reasons: that he is useful; that he is pleasant; and above all, that he is good, that is, rational and virtuous. Friendships founded on goodness are associated not only with earthly benefits, but also with higher goods such as companionship, dependability, and trust.

For Plato, the best kind of friendship is that which lovers have for each other. It is a philia born out of eros, and that in turn feeds back into eros to strengthen and develop it, transforming it from a lust for possession into a shared desire for a higher level of understanding of the self, the other, and the world.

In short, philia transforms eros from a lust for possession into an impulse for philosophy.

Real friends seek together to live truer, fuller lives by relating to each other authentically and teaching each other about the limitations of their beliefs and the defects in their character, which are a far greater source of error than mere rational confusion: they are, in effect, each other's therapist—and in that much it helps to find a friend with some degree of openness, articulacy, and insight, both to change and to be changed.

3. Storge

Storge ['store-jay'], or familial love, is a kind of philia pertaining to the love between parents and their children. It differs from most philia in that it tends, especially with younger children, to be unilateral or asymmetrical. More broadly, storge is the fondness or attachment that is born out of familiarity or dependency. Unlike eros and philia, it is not particularly predicated on our personal qualities.

People in the early stages of a romantic liaison often expect unconditional storge, but find only the need and dependency of eros, and, if they are lucky, the maturity and fertility of philia.

But given enough time, eros tends to mutate into storge.

4. Agape

Agape ['aga-pay'] is universal love, such as the love for strangers, nature, or God.

Unlike storge, agape does not depend on nearby filiation or familiarity.

Also called charity by Christian thinkers, agape can be said to encompass the modern concept of altruism, as defined as unselfish concern for the welfare of others.

Recent studies link altruism with a number of benefits. In the short-term, an altruistic act leaves us with a euphoric feeling, the so-called 'helper's high'. In the longer term, altruism has been associated with better mental and physical health, and even greater longevity.

At a social level, altruism serves as a signal of cooperative intentions, and also of resource availability and so of mating or partnering potential. It also opens up a debt account, encouraging beneficiaries to reciprocate with gifts and favours that may be of much greater value to us than those with which we felt able to part.

More generally, altruism, or agape, helps to build and maintain the psychological, social, and, indeed, environmental fabric that shields, sustains, and enriches us.

Given the increasing anger and division in our society, and the state of our planet, we could all do with quite a bit more agape.

5. Ludus

Ludus is playful or uncommitted love.

Ludus can involve activities such as teasing and dancing, or more overt flirting, seducing, and conjugating. The focus is on fun, and sometimes also on conquest, with no strings attached.

Ludic relationships are casual, undemanding, and uncomplicated, but, for all that, can be very long-lasting.

Ludus works best when both parties are mature and self-sufficient.

Problems arise when one party mistakes ludus for eros, whereas ludus is, in fact, much more compatible with philia.

The key to ludus is not to lose your head.

6. Pragma

Pragma is a kind of practical love founded on reason or duty and one's longer-term interests. Sexual attraction takes a back seat in favour of personal qualities and compatibilities, shared goals, and 'making it work'.

In the days of arranged marriages, pragma must have been very common. Although unfashionable, and at a polar opposite of romantic love, it remains widespread, most visibly in certain high-profile celebrity and political pairings.

Many relationships that start off as eros or ludus end up as various combinations of storge and pragma.

Pragma may seem opposed to ludus, but the two can sometimes co-exist with the one providing a counterpoint to the other. In the best of cases, the partners in the pragma relationship agree to turn a blind eye—or even a sympathetic eye, as with Simone de Beauvoir and Jean-Paul Sartre, or Vita Sackville-West and Harold Nicholson.

7. Philautia

Philautia, finally, is self-love, which can be healthy or unhealthy.

Unhealthy self-love is akin to *hubris*. In Ancient Greece, people could be accused of hubris if they placed themselves above the gods, or, like certain modern politicians, above the greater good. Many people believed that hubris led to destruction, or *nemesis*.

In modern English, hubris has come to mean an inflated sense of one's status, abilities, or accomplishments, especially when accompanied by haughtiness or arrogance. Because it does not accord with the truth, hubris promotes injustice, conflict, and enmity.

Healthy self-love, on the other hand, is akin to self-esteem, which is our cognitive and, above all, emotional appraisal of our own worth. More than that, it is the matrix through which we think, feel, and act, and reflects on our relation to ourselves, to others, and to the world.

In everyday English, 'self-esteem' and 'self-confidence' tend to be used interchangeably. But they are different constructs that do not always go hand in hand. In particular, it is possible to be highly self-confident and yet to have profoundly low self-esteem, as is the case, for example, with many performers and celebrities.

People with healthy self-esteem do not need to prop themselves up with externals such as income, status, or notoriety, or lean on crutches such as alcohol, drugs, or sex.

They are able to invest themselves completely in projects and people because they do not fear failure or rejection.

Of course, they suffer hurt and disappointment, but their setbacks neither damage nor diminish them.

Owing to their resilience, they are open to growth experiences and relationships, tolerant of risk, quick to joy and delight, and accepting and forgiving of themselves and others.

In closing, there is, of course, a kind of porosity between the seven types of love, which keep on seeping and passing into one another.

For Plato, love aims at beautiful and good things, because the possession of beautiful and good things is called happiness, and happiness is an end-in-itself.

Of all good and beautiful things, the best, most beautiful, and most dependable is truth or wisdom, which is why Plato called love not a god but a philosopher.

Notes

- Plato, *Symposium*. 'He whom love touches not walks in darkness.'
- G Flaubert (1856), *Madame Bovary*.
- Homer, *Iliad*.
- Bible, OT, Genesis 22. Bible, OT, 1 and 2 Samuel.
- Bible, OT, Ruth.
- JA Lee (1973), *Colors of Love*.
- Homer, *Iliad*.
- Sophocles, *Antigone*, 887-889.

- A Schopenhauer (1819), *The World as Will and Representation*.
- Aristotle, *Nicomachean Ethics*, Bk. 10.
- Plato, *Symposium*.
- Plato, *Phædrus*.
- Plato, *Symposium*.

8

HOW TO WIN

Silence is a source of great strength.

— Lao Tzu

Love and agape are all fine and dandy, but sometimes people can injure us.

Insults and put-downs can damage our prospects and happiness by undermining our self-confidence and self-esteem. Even casual denigration (so called microaggressions) can, over time, lead to feelings of loneliness, alienation, anger, anxiety, and depression.

Insults can be physical, such as hitting, slapping, or spitting. But more usually, they are verbal—whether direct or indirect.

Examples of indirect verbal insults are jokes, ironic comments, backhanded compliments, mimicry, and false fascination.

Facial expressions can substitute for speech, and things like a cold or constant stare, a false or exaggerated smile, or a raised eyebrow, depending on their intention, can also count as indirect verbal insults.

All of the above involve some kind of positive action, and are therefore insults of commission. But insults of omission are equally if not more common.

Examples of insults of omission are not inviting or including someone, not deferring to their age or rank, and not responding to their friendly openings, including basic eye contact.

Xenophobia, I have found, is when you smile at people and they don't smile back.

~

How to give as good as you get

So, what's the best way of dealing with all these different kinds of insult and injury?

Consider these six possible responses, and then we'll go through each one in turn.

1. Anger.
2. Acceptance.
3. Returning the insult.
4. Humour.
5. Ignoring the insult.
6. Rebuking the insulter.

Which of the six responses do you think is the weakest, and which the strongest?

1. Anger

Anger is a very weak response, and this for three main reasons:

- It shows that we take the insult, and therefore the insulter, seriously.
- It suggests that there may be some truth in the insult.
- It upsets and destabilizes us, which, apart from being unpleasant, can invite further insults.

2. Acceptance

Acceptance may seem weak but can be the strongest response of all. Hear me out.

When someone insults us, we ought to consider three things: whether the insult is true, who it came from, and why.

If the insult is true or mostly true, the person it came from is reasonable, and his or her motive is worthy, then the insult is not an insult but a statement of fact, and, moreover, one that could be very helpful to us.

Hence, we seldom take offence at our parents, teachers, or friends, who, by telling us the truth, are trying to help rather than hinder or harm us.

More generally, if you respect the person who has insulted you, you ought, instead of getting angry or upset, to give thought to the 'insult' and learn as much as you can from it.

On the other hand, if you think that the person who insulted you is unworthy of you and your cares, you have no reason to take offence, just as you have no reason to take offence at a naughty child or a barking dog.

So, whatever the case, you have no reason to take offence.

3. Returning the insult

There are a number of issues with returning the insult. First, your riposte has to be clever and cutting, or at least apt; and, second, it has to occur to you at just the right moment.

L'esprit de l'escalier in French or *Treppenwitz* in German ['staircase wit'] refers to the common experience of thinking too late of the perfect put-down. But even if we are as quick-witted and sharp-tongued as an Oscar Wilde or George Bernard Shaw, the perfect put-down is seldom the best response.

The fundamental problem with the put-down, however sparkling it may be, is that it equalizes us with our insulter, bringing them up to our level and us down to theirs. This gives them, their behaviour, and their insult far too much legitimacy.

Returning the insult also risks injuring the insulter (who, in all probability, is fairly fragile) and inviting further attacks.

The witty put-down does have a place, but only among friends, to add to the merriment. And it ought to be followed by a token of reconciliation such as a toast or a pat on the shoulder.

In other words, the witty put-down should only ever be used for humour, when it is also at its most effective.

4. Humour

Cato the Younger, the Roman statesman and stoic philosopher, was pleading a case when his adversary Lentulus spat in his face. After wiping off the spittle, Cato said: 'I will swear to anyone, Lentulus, that people are wrong to say that you cannot use your mouth.'

George Bernard Shaw, it is said, once invited Winston Churchill to his new play. The card read: 'I am enclosing two tickets to the first night of my new play; bring a friend—if you have one.' Churchill replied: 'Cannot possibly attend first night; will attend second—if there is one.'

Here's a third example, just for the fun: The American actress Ilka Chase wrote a number of novels. One day, an anonymous actress said to her: 'I enjoyed reading your book. Who wrote it for you?' To which Chase replied: 'Darling, I'm so glad that you liked it. Who read it to you?'

Humour, if successful, can be a very effective response, and this for three main reasons:

- It completely undercuts the insulter and his or her insult.
- It brings any third parties on side.
- It diffuses the tension of the situation.

A similar strategy is to go with the insult and even add to it, for example: 'Ah, if you knew me better, you would find greater fault still!' This makes a mockery of the insult and, by extension, of the insulter.

In Edmond Rostand's play, *Cyrano de Bergerac* (1897), the Viscount de Valvert seeks to insult Cyrano by telling him that his nose is 'very big'. Cyrano responds, 'Very! ... Is that all?' 'Ah no! young blade! That was a trifle short! You might have said at least a hundred things by varying the tone...'

Cyrano then improvises a long list of more imaginative insults, including, 'Sir, if I had such a nose I'd amputate it!' and 'Be careful when you bow your head or you might lose your balance and fall over.'

According to the stage directions, Valvert is left 'choking with rage'.

5. Ignoring the insult

Humour, unfortunately, has some of the same drawbacks as returning the insult: Your riposte has to be funny, and it has to be well-timed and well delivered.

Ignoring the insult is much easier, and, in fact, more powerful.

One day, a boor struck Cato while he was out at the public baths. When the boor realized who he had struck, he came to apologize. Instead of getting angry or accepting the apology, Cato replied: 'I don't remember being struck.'

Subtext: 'You are so insignificant to me that I don't even care to register your apology, let alone take offence at your insult.'

6. Rebuking the insulter

Ignoring the insult works well with strangers, but may not be a sensible or viable strategy when it comes to people with whom we have an ongoing personal or professional relationship.

In such cases, it may be preferable to 'have a quiet word' (quiet, but firm) in a bid to reinforce our boundaries. Let me explain.

To create a healthy sense of professional or personal space, we tend to set certain physical and psychological boundaries. It is vital to be clear about where these boundaries lie, and, as with puppy training, to religiously reassert them each and every time they are crossed.

Establishing and maintaining boundaries can take a lot of thought and effort, and sometimes courage too, but, if done from the beginning, is usually very effective, and very quickly so.

In closing, we need never take offence at an insult.

Offence exists not in the insult or the insulter but in our reaction to them, and our reactions are completely within our control.

It is unreasonable to expect a boor to be anything but a boor; if we take offence at his bad behaviour, we have only ourselves to blame.

9

HOW TO PARTY

Men die in despair, while spirits die in ecstasy.

— Honoré de Balzac

And now it's time to part-ay, to celebrate life, to feel alive to our very core.

But, let's be honest, the parties of today are nothing like they used to be...

To commemorate the destruction of the bloodthirsty lioness Sekhmet, the Ancient Egyptians held communal Festivals of Drunkenness at the beginning of their calendar year in mid-August, when the Nile is swelling. Revellers drank to the point of passing out, only to be awoken by the beating of drums.

The celebrations, which typically took place in and around temples and shrines, also included dancing and public sex, in part to imitate and propitiate the flood and fertility to come.

The word 'orgy', which ultimately derives from the Greek *orgion*, entered the English language in the 1560s to mean 'a licentious revelry'.

Today, people think of an orgy as a party involving open and unrestrained sex between multiple participants.

But originally, *orgia* referred to the secret rites of Ancient Greek mystery cults such as the Dionysian Mysteries and the Cult of Cybele, which aimed, above all, at ecstatic union with the divine.

Dionysus, who, like Jesus, died and was reborn, was the god of wine, regeneration, fertility, theatre, and religious ecstasy. He was a very important god—no doubt, in certain periods and places, the most important—and most fervently celebrated around the time of the vernal equinox.

Let me paint you a picture of a Dionysian orgy.

The procession begins at sunset, led by torchbearers followed by wine and fruit bearers, musicians, and a throng of revellers wearing masks and... well, not much else. At the rear is a giant phallus representing the resurrection of the twice-born god. Everyone is pushing and shoving, singing and dancing, and shouting the name of the god mixed in with ribaldry and obscenities.

Arriving at a clearing in the woods, the crowd goes wild with drinking, dancing, and every imaginable manner of sex. The god is in the wine, and to imbibe it is to be possessed by his spirit—although in the bull's horn the booze has been interlaced with a number of other entheogens (substances which 'generate the divine from within'). Animals, which stand in for the god, are hunted down, ripped apart with bare hands, and consumed raw with the blood still warm and dripping.

Figure 6. Bacchus and Ariadne, by Titian (c. 1520). National Gallery, London.

This 'Dionysian' impulse for irrationality and chaos can be understood as a natural inversion of, and release from, the habitual 'Apollonian' order and restraint imposed by the state and state religion.

In the *Birth of Tragedy* (1872), the philosopher Friedrich Nietzsche recognized the Dionysian impulse as a primal and universal force:

> Either through the influence of narcotic drink, of which all primitive men and peoples speak, or through the powerful coming on of spring, which drives joyfully through all of nature, that Dionysian excitement arises. As its power

> increases, the subjective fades into complete forgetfulness of self. In the German Middle Ages under the same power of Dionysus constantly growing hordes waltzed from place to place, singing and dancing. In that St John's and St Vitus's dance we recognize the Bacchic chorus of the Greeks once again, and its precursors in Asia Minor, right back to Babylon and the orgiastic Sacæa.

By diverting the Dionysian impulse into special rites on special days, the orgy kept it under control, preventing it from surfacing in more insidious and perfidious ways.

More than that, it transmutated it into an invigorating and liberating, and, in that much, profoundly religious, celebration of life and the life force.

The orgy permitted people to escape from their artificial and restricted social roles and regress into a more authentic state of nature, which modern psychologists have come to associate with the Freudian id or unconscious.

It appealed most to marginal groups, since it set aside the usual hierarchies of man over woman, master over slave, patrician over commoner, rich over poor, and citizen over foreigner.

In short, it gave people a much-needed break: like modern holidays, but cheaper and more effective.

~

The Dionysian cult spread through the Greek colonies to Rome.

In 186 BCE, the Roman Senate severely restricted it, but illicit Bacchanalia persisted, especially in Southern Italy, gradually folding into the much tamer Liberalia in honour of Liber Pater

('Free Father'), the Roman god of wine and fertility who so resembled Bacchus/Dionysus as, eventually, to fuse with him.

As with the Dionysian cult, the Liberalia featured a giant phallus, carted through the countryside to fertilize the land and safeguard crops—after which a virtuous Roman matron would crown the phallus with a garland or wreath.

This sort of 'depravity' also featured in other Roman religious festivals such as the Floralia and the Lupercalia. The Lupercalia, for example, involved, among others, naked noblemen coursing through the streets and whipping willing ladies with strips of goatskin.

The fourth-century reign of Constantius II marked the beginning of the formal persecution of paganism by the now Christian Roman Empire. But the springtime fertility orgy survived through the tumults of the centuries, albeit in attenuated forms.

At last, unable to do away with it, the Church integrated it into its calendar as Carnival—which, to this day, involves reversal of social norms and roles, licentiousness, and feasting ahead of the deprivations of Lent.

May Day celebrations across Europe and North America trace their origins to the Roman Floralia and corresponding Celtic traditions.

In mediæval times, people danced around the gigantic phallic symbol of the Maypole before descending into the fields or forests for wanton sex, avowedly to 'fertilize the land'.

In 1644, the Puritans outlawed Maypoles in England, with the Long Parliament's ordinance damning them as 'a Heathenish vanity, generally abused to superstition and wickedness'.

'Ecstasy' [*ex-stasis*] literally means 'to be or stand outside oneself'.

It is a trance-like state in which consciousness of an object is so heightened that the subject dissolves or merges into the object.

Albert Einstein called it the 'mystic emotion' and spoke of it as 'the finest emotion of which we are capable', 'the germ of all art and all true science', and 'the core of the true religious sentiment'.

Far more than ever before, modern society emphasizes the sovereign supremacy of the ego and the ultimate separateness and responsibility of each and every one of us.

From a young age, we are taught to remain in tight control of our ego or persona with the aim of projecting it as far out as possible.

As a result, we have lost the art of letting go—and indeed, may no longer even recognize the possibility—leading to a poverty or monotony of lived experience.

Letting go can threaten the life that we have built and even the person that we have become, but it can also free us from our modern narrowness and neediness, and deliver, or re-deliver, us into a bigger and brighter world.

Just for the record, I am not advocating drug-fuelled orgies or anything of the sort, but merely suggesting that we could greatly benefit, both as individuals and as a society, from acknowledging and embracing our darker side—or what the psychiatrist Carl Jung called our 'shadow'.

If left neglected, our shadow can acquire a life of its own, threatening to undermine us and those around us.

In Robert Louis Stevenson's *The Strange Case of Dr Jekyll and Mr Hyde* (1886), Dr Jekyll attempts to destroy his shadow, but in so doing mutates into the hideous Mr Hyde.

As Mr Hyde, he murders Sir Danvers Carew, a handsome and congenial Member of Parliament.

Now a hunted outlaw, Dr Jekyll/Mr Hyde goes into hiding and ends up taking his own life.

Many of us have a fascination for supervillains such as the Joker who are so completely overrun by their shadow as to be nothing but sheer darkness.

In the film *The Dark Knight*, the Joker says:

> Introduce a little anarchy. Upset the established order, and everything becomes chaos. I'm an agent of chaos...

But despite the strong feeling that he evokes, the Joker is a flat, one-dimensional character—as, indeed, is his nemesis, the boring Batman.

Rather than aim at the one or succumb to the other, we should seek to unite the Apollonian and the Dionysian—and, like the Ancient Greeks, realize the ever-receding dream of civilization.

5 ways to explore your darker side

1. Be tolerant of yourself. You are human, and, like it or not, contain every human aspect and impulse. Instead of approving of certain aspects and disapproving of others, try to acknowledge and accept them all. It is only by accepting a hitherto rejected aspect that you can begin to understand and control it, and—who knows?—maybe even enjoy and exploit it.

2. Let your feelings flow. Instead of repressing or censuring your feelings, seek to express and explore them in thought and conversation, and through dreaming, writing, and art or creativity. For instance, keep a diary at your bedside in which you record and interpret those dreams that you are able to remember. In *General Aspects of Dream Psychology* (1916), Jung argued that dreams contribute to the self-regulation of the psyche by automatically bringing up everything that is repressed, neglected, or unknown.

3. Listen to your feelings, especially the difficult or distressing ones. I once treated a patient who seemed to have the 'perfect' life: a successful career, a dutiful husband, a beautiful child... But, tragically, she felt like a prisoner in that life. Because she could not admit this to herself, she became increasingly depressed, to the point of hearing voices and cutting her wrists. After several months in hospital, she came to realize that she wanted, or needed, a divorce, and, gradually, her depression began to lift. The feelings we least want to heed are often the ones that we most need to heed.

4. Observe and learn from your reactions to others. If you find yourself vehemently opposed to something in someone, there's a good chance that that something is also in you, or, at least, corresponds to something in you. For example, if you get angry at someone for being loose and lecherous, or 'acting like a whore', there may well be a repressed part of lust or jealousy in you. As Jung said, 'Everything that irritates us about others can lead us to an understanding of ourselves.'

5. Cultivate idleness and boredom. We often tell ourselves that we work hard from a desire for idleness. But in fact, we find even short periods of idleness hard to bear. Faced with a traffic jam, we prefer to make a detour even if the alternative route is likely to take longer than sitting through the traffic. Our problem with idleness is that it can quickly turn to boredom, opening the gates on some very uncomfortable thoughts and feelings that we normally block out with a flurry of activity or with the opposite thoughts and feelings—like Virginia Woolf's Mrs Dalloway, 'always giving parties to cover the silence.'

But if we can sit squarely and comfortably with our shadow, we won't need to run around anymore, or treat people badly, or suffer so much.

Notes

- F Nietzsche (1872), *The Birth of Tragedy*, Ch. 1. Trans. Ian Johnston.
- Livy, *History of Rome*, 39.18.
- A Einstein, as quoted in P Barker and CG Shugart (1981), *After Einstein: Proceedings of the Einstein Centennial Celebration*, p179. Memphis State University Press.
- RL Stevenson (1886), *The Strange Case of Dr Jekyll and Mr Hyde*.
- C Nolan (2008), *The Dark Knight*.
- CG Jung (1916), *General Aspects of Dream Psychology*, 30:483.
- V Woolf (1925), *Mrs Dalloway*.

10

HOW TO THINK

> If you know your enemies and know yourself, you will not be imperilled in a hundred battles.
>
> — Sun Tzu

Following his defeat at the Battle of Actium in 31 BCE, Marc Antony heard a rumour that Cleopatra had committed suicide and, in consequence, stabbed himself in the abdomen—only to discover that Cleopatra herself had been responsible for spreading the rumour.

He later died in her arms.

'Fake news' is nothing new, but in our Internet age it has spread like a contagious disease, swinging elections, fomenting social unrest, undermining institutions, and diverting political capital away from health, education, the environment, and all-round good government.

So how best to guard against it?

As a medical specialist, I've spent over twenty years in formal education. With the possible exception of my two-year masters in philosophy, the emphasis of my education has always been firmly and squarely on fact accumulation.

Today, I have little use for most of these facts, and though I am only middle-aged, many are already out of date, or highly questionable.

But what I do rely on—every day, all the time—is my faculty for critical thinking. As BF Skinner once put it, 'Education is what survives when what has been learnt has been forgotten.'

But can critical thinking even be taught?

In Plato's *Meno*, Socrates says that people with wisdom and virtue are very poor at imparting those qualities: Themistocles, the Athenian politician and general, was able to teach his son Cleophantus skills such as standing upright on horseback and shooting javelins, but no one ever credited Cleophantus with anything like his father's wisdom; and the same could also be said of Lysimachus and his son Aristides, and Thucydides and his sons Melesias and Stephanus.

In Plato's *Protagoras*, Socrates says that Pericles, who led Athens at the peak of its golden age, gave his sons excellent instruction in everything that could be learnt from teachers, but when it came to wisdom, he simply left them to 'wander at their own free will in a sort of hope that they would light upon virtue of their own accord'.

It may be that wisdom and virtue cannot be taught (though we did have a stab at wisdom in Chapter 4), but thinking skills certainly can—or, at least, the beginning of them.

So rather than leaving thinking skills to chance, why not make more time for them in our schools and universities, and be more rigorous and systematic about them?

I'll make a start by introducing you to what I have called 'the five enemies of rational thought':

1. Formal fallacy.
2. Informal fallacy.
3. Cognitive bias.
4. Cognitive distortion.
5. Self-deception.

Let's go through each one in turn, with a special focus on the mightiest of them all, self-deception.

1. Formal fallacy

A fallacy is some kind of defect in an argument.

A formal fallacy is an invalid type of argument. It is a deductive argument with an invalid form, for example:

> Some A are B.
> Some B are C.
> Therefore, some A are C.

If you cannot yet see that this argument is invalid, substitute A, B, and C with 'insects', 'herbivores', and 'mammals'.

Insects, clearly, are not mammals!

A formal fallacy is built into the structure of an argument and is invalid irrespective of the content of the argument.

2. Informal fallacy

An informal fallacy, in contrast, is one that can only be identified through an analysis of the content of the argument.

Informal fallacies often turn on the misuse of language, for example, using a key term or phrase in an ambiguous way, with one meaning in one part of the argument and another meaning in another part—called 'fallacy of equivocation'.

Informal fallacies can also distract from the weakness of an argument, or appeal to the emotions instead of reason.

Here are a few more examples of informal fallacies.

Damning the alternatives: Arguing in favour of something by damning its alternatives.

> *Tim's useless and Bob's a drunk. So, I'll marry Jimmy. Jimmy's the right man for me.*

Gambler's fallacy: Assuming that the outcome of one or more independent events can impact the outcome of a subsequent independent event.

> *June is pregnant with her fourth child. Her first three children are all boys, so this time it's bound to be a girl.*

Appeal to popularity: Concluding the truth of a proposition on the basis that most or many people believe it to be true.

> *Of course he's guilty: even his mother has turned her back on him.*

Argument from ignorance: Upholding the truth of a proposition based on a lack of evidence against it, or the falsity of a proposition based on a lack of evidence for it.

Scientists haven't found any evidence of current or past life on Mars. So, we can be certain that there has never been any life on Mars.

Argument to moderation: Arguing that the moderate view or middle position must be the right or best one.

Half the country favours leaving the European Union, the other half favours remaining. Let's compromise by leaving the European Union but remaining in the Customs Union.

If you're interested, I have many more examples of informal fallacy in *Hypersanity: Thinking Beyond Thinking*.

3. Cognitive bias

Cognitive bias is sloppy, if not necessarily faulty, reasoning: a mental shortcut or heuristic intended to spare us time, effort, or discomfort—often while reinforcing our self-image or world-view—but at the cost of accuracy or reliability.

For example, in explaining the behaviour of other people, our tendency is to overestimate the role of character traits over situational factors—a bias, called correspondence bias, that goes into reverse when it comes to explaining our own behaviour. Thus, if Charlotte fails to mow the lawn, I indict her with forgetfulness, laziness, or spite; but if I fail to mow the lawn, I absolve myself on the grounds of busyness, tiredness, or inclement weather.

Another important cognitive bias is my-side, or confirmation, bias, which is the propensity to search for or recall only those stories, facts, and arguments that are in keeping with our pre-existing beliefs while filtering out those that conflict with them—which, especially on social media, can lead us to inhabit a so-called echo chamber.

4. Cognitive distortion

Cognitive distortion is a concept from cognitive-behavioural therapy (CBT), developed by psychiatrist Aaron Beck in the 1960s and used in the treatment of depression and other mental disorders.

Cognitive distortion involves interpreting events and situations so that they conform to and reinforce our outlook or frame of mind, typically on the basis of very scant or partial evidence, or even no evidence at all.

Common cognitive distortions in depression include selective abstraction and catastrophic thinking.

Selective abstraction is to focus on a single and often insignificant negative event or condition to the exclusion of other, more positive ones, for example, 'My partner hates me. He gave me an annoyed look three days ago.'

Catastrophic thinking is to exaggerate and dramatize the likely consequences of an event or situation, for example, 'The pain in my knee is getting worse. When I'm reduced to a wheelchair, I won't be able to go to work and pay the bills. So, I'll end up losing my house and dying in the street.'

A cognitive distortion can open up a vicious circle, with the cognitive distortion feeding the depression, and the depression the cognitive distortion.

Cognitive distortion as broadly understood is not limited to depression and other mental disorders, but is also a feature of, among others, poor self-esteem, jealousy, and marital conflict.

5. Self-deception

Of the five enemies of rational thought, the most important by far is self-deception, because it tends to underlie all the others.

If we do not think clearly, if we cannot see the wood for the trees, this is not usually because we lack intelligence or education or experience, but because we feel exposed and vulnerable —and rather than come to terms with a painful truth, prefer, almost reflexively, to deceive and defend ourselves.

All self-deception, I think, can be understood in terms of ego defence. In psychoanalytic theory, ego defences are unconscious processes that we deploy to diffuse the fear and anxiety that arise when who we think we are or who we think we ought to be (our conscious 'superego') comes into conflict with who we really are (our unconscious 'id').

For instance, at an unconscious level a man may find himself physically attracted to another man, but at a conscious level he may find such an attraction flatly unacceptable. To diffuse the anxiety or tension that arises from this conflict, he may deploy one or more ego defences.

For example, (1) he might refuse to admit to himself that he is attracted to a man. Or (2) he might superficially adopt attitudes that are diametrically opposed to those of a stereotypical homosexual, such as going out for several pints with the lads, banging his fists on the counter, and peppering his speech with loud profanities. Or (3) he might transfer his attraction onto someone else and then berate *him* for being gay.

In each case, the man has used a common ego defence, respectively, (1) repression, (2) reaction formation, and (3) projection.

Repression can be thought of as 'motivated forgetting': the active, albeit unconscious, 'forgetting' of unacceptable drives, emotions, and ideas. Repression is often confused with denial, which is the refusal to admit to uncomfortable aspects of reality. But whereas repression relates to mental or internal stimuli, denial relates to external stimuli, to things that are 'out there'.

Reaction formation is the superficial adoption—and, often, exaggeration—of emotions and impulses that are diametrically opposed to one's own. A possible high-profile case of reaction formation is that of a certain US congressman, who, as chairman of the Missing and Exploited Children's Caucus, introduced legislation to protect children from exploitation by adults over the Internet. The congressman resigned when it later emerged that he had been exchanging sexually explicit messages with a teenage boy.

Projection can be defined as the attribution of one's unacceptable thoughts, feelings, and impulses to others. Examples of projection include the envious person who believes that everyone envies her, the person with fantasies of infidelity who is convinced that her partner is cheating on her, and the covetous person who lives in constant fear of being dispossessed.

Just as common as projection is splitting, which is the division or polarization of beliefs and people into good and bad by selectively focusing on either their positive or negative attributes. This is often seen in politics, for instance, when left-wingers paint right-wingers as selfish and narrow-minded, and right-wingers paint left-wingers as hypocritical and irresponsible— or, nowadays, 'deplorables' and 'elites'. Splitting diffuses the anxiety that arises from our inability to grasp a complex and nuanced state of affairs by simplifying and schematizing it and making it easier to process.

Similar to splitting is idealization, which involves overestimating the positive attributes of a person, object, or idea, while at the same time underestimating its negative attributes. A paradigm of idealization is infatuation, when love is confused with the need to love, and the idealized person's negative attributes are glossed over or even painted as positive. Though it can make for a rude awakening, there are few better ways of relieving our existential anxiety than by manufacturing something that is 'perfect' for us, be it a piece of equipment, a place, country, person, or god.

If in love with someone inaccessible, it might be more convenient to intellectualize our love, maybe even by thinking about it in terms of idealization! In intellectualization, uncomfortable feelings associated with a problem are repressed by thinking about the problem in cold or abstract terms. I once received a phone call from a junior doctor in psychiatry in which he described a recent in-patient admission as 'a 47-year-old mother of two who attempted to cessate her life as a result of being diagnosed with a metastatic mitotic lesion'. A formulation such as '...who tried to kill herself after being told that she is dying of cancer' would have been far better English, but all too effective at evoking the full horror of this poor lady's predicament.

Intellectualization should not be confused with rationalization, which is the use of feeble but seemingly plausible arguments either to justify something that is painful to accept ('sour grapes') or to make it seem 'not so bad after all' ('sweet lemons'). For example, a person who has been rejected by a love interest might convince himself that she rejected him because she did not share in his ideal of happiness (sour grapes); and also that her rejection is a blessing in disguise insofar as it has freed him to find someone more suitable (sweet lemons).

While no one can altogether avoid using ego defences, some ego defences are considered more 'mature' than others: not only because they involve some degree of insight, but also because they can be adaptive or useful.

If a person is angry at his boss, he might go home and kick the dog, or he might instead go out and play a good game of tennis. The first instance (kicking the dog) is an example of displacement, the redirection of uncomfortable feelings towards someone or something less important, which is clearly an immature ego defence. The second instance (playing a good game of tennis) is an example of sublimation, the channelling of uncomfortable feelings into socially condoned or productive activities, which is a much more mature ego defence.

There are a number of mature ego defences like sublimation that can be substituted for the more primitive ones.

Altruism, for instance, can in some cases be a form of sublimation in which we deal with our anxiety by stepping outside ourselves and helping others. By concentrating on the needs of others, people in altruistic vocations such as doctoring, nursing, and teaching may be able to permanently push their own needs into the background. Conversely, people who care for a disabled or elderly person may experience profound anxiety and distress when this role is suddenly removed from them.

Another mature ego defence is humour. By seeing the absurd or ridiculous aspect of an emotion, event, or situation, we are able to look at it in a less threatening light. If we, human beings, laugh so much, it is no doubt because we have the most developed unconscious in the animal kingdom. The things that we laugh about the most are: our errors and inadequacies; the difficult challenges that we face around personal identity, social relationships, and death; and incongruity, absurdity, and meaninglessness. These are all deeply human concerns: Just as no one has ever seen a laughing dog, so no one has ever heard of a laughing god.

Further up the maturity scale is asceticism, which is the denial of the importance of that which most people fear or strive for, and so of the very grounds for anxiety and depression. If fear is, ultimately, for oneself, then the denial of the self removes the very grounds for fear. People in modern societies such as ours are much more anxious than people in traditional or historical societies, no doubt because of the strong emphasis that modern societies place on the self as an independent and autonomous agent, that is, as an ego or 'I'.

In the Hindu *Bhagavad Gita*, the god Krishna appears to the archer Arjuna in the midst of the Battle of Kurukshetra and advises him not to succumb to his scruples about killing his enemy cousins, the Kauravas, but do his duty and fight on.

In either case, all the men on the battle are one day destined to die, as are all men. Their deaths are trivial, because the spirit within them, their human essence, does not depend on their individual incarnations for its continued existence.

Krishna says, 'When one sees eternity in things that pass away and infinity in finite things, then one has pure knowledge.'

> There has never been a time when you and I have not existed, nor will there be a time when we will cease to exist ... the wise are not deluded by these changes.

There are a great number of ego defences, and the combinations and circumstances in which we use them are a function and reflection of our personality. Indeed, one could go so far as to argue that the self is nothing but the sum of its ego defences, which are constantly molding, maintaining, protecting, and repairing it.

The self is like a cracked mask that is in constant need of being pieced together. But behind the mask there is nobody at home.

While we cannot entirely escape from ego defences, we can gain some insight into how we use them. This self-knowledge, if we have the courage for it, can awaken us to ourselves, to others, and to the world around us, and free us to achieve our full potential as human beings.

The greatest oracle of the ancient world was the Oracle at Delphi, and there, inscribed on the forecourt of the temple of Apollo, was a simple two-word command:

> Γνῶθι σεαυτόν
>
> Know thyself.

How to tell when you're deceiving yourself

By its very nature, self-deception is hard to distinguish from the truth—whether our internal, emotional truth, or the external, objective truth.

You have to develop and trust your intuition, and ask yourself: What does it feel like to react in the way that I'm reacting? Does it feel calm, considered, and nuanced, or shallow and knee-jerk? Am I taking the welfare of others into consideration, or is it just all about me? Am I satisfied with, even proud of, my self-conquering effort, or am I left feeling small, anxious, or ashamed?

Self-deception doesn't 'add up' in the grand scheme of things and can easily be brought down by even superficial questioning. As with a jigsaw, try to look at the bigger picture of your life and see how the thought or reaction might fit in. Did you react from a position of strength or vulnerability? What would the person you most respect think? What would Socrates or the

Dalai Lama think? Talk to other people and gather their opinions. If they disagree with you, does that make you feel angry, upset, or defensive? The coherence of your reaction speaks volumes about the character of your motives.

Finally, truth is constructive and adaptive, while lies are destructive and self-defeating. So how useful is a self-deceptive thought or reaction going to be for you? Are you just covering up an irrational fear, or helping to create a solid foundation for the future? Are you empowering yourself to fulfil your highest potential, or depriving yourself of opportunities for growth and creating further problems down the line?

Is the cycle simply going to repeat itself, or will the truth, at last, make you free?

Notes

- Sun Tzu, *The Art of War*, Ch. 3. 'If you know your enemies and know yourself, you will not be imperilled in a hundred battles.'
- BF Skinner (1965), *Review lecture: The technology of teaching*. Proceedings of the Royal Society of London: Series B, Biological Sciences 162(989):427-443.
- Plato, *Meno*.
- Plato, *Protagoras*.
- *The Bhagavad Gita*, 18:20-22.
- *The Bhagavad Gita*, 2:12-13.

THE SECRET TO EVERYTHING

I hope you've enjoyed the journey so far.

Have you found the common thread that runs through all the chapters?

Let's briefly summarise the key insights from each chapter.

In Chapter 1, *How to see*, we discussed how contemplative activities such as gardening and birdwatching can remove us from our tortured heads and reconnect us with something much greater and higher than our personal problems and preoccupations.

In Chapter 2, *How to dream*, we saw how the little death of sleep helps us to live. In particular, dreams, by breaking down boundaries, enable us to assimilate experiences, process emotions, and generate and test ideas. I also confided that I used to have trouble sleeping: But now I can fall asleep on demand simply by clearing my mind.

In Chapter 3, *How to be religious*, we talked about gratitude, which is the method that I use to clear my mind. Like gardening, gratitude turns us outward and away from our problems and preoccupations. More than that, by shifting our focus from what we strive for to all that we already have, it broadens our perspectives and frees us to live life, no longer for ourselves, but for life itself.

In Chapter 4, *How to be wise*, we worked out that wisdom is not so much a kind of knowledge as a way of seeing, or ways of seeing. Wisdom is the understanding of the right relations between things, which calls for more distant and removed perspectives, and also the ability or flexibility to shift between different perspectives.

In Chapter 5, *How to be fearless*, it transpired that the root cause of all anxiety is the fear of death. By coming to terms with death, we can alleviate our anxiety and, more than that, free ourselves to self-actualize—that is, stretch beyond our individual, limited selves and fulfil our true potential as human beings.

In Chapter 6, *How to live*, we asked about the meaning of life. We concluded that, whatever the case, we are better off creating our own meaning or meanings—because unless we do, our lives may have, at worst, no meaning at all, and, at best, only some unfathomable meaning that is not of our own choosing. According to Viktor Frankl, we can give our life meaning in a number of ways, all of which involve turning outward and away from ourselves.

In Chapter 7, *How to love*, we looked at how romantic love came to take the place of religion in lending meaning to our lives. But I warned that, by chasing romantic love, we run the risk of being disappointed, and of passing over other types of love that may prove more stable and fulfilling. Love ought to be about the other, and turn us outward, whereas romantic love is mostly about ourselves—whence the melodrama.

In Chapter 8, *How to win*, we concluded that, in most cases, the best way to deal with an insult is simply to ignore it. Because we are egocentric and insecure beings, we tend to take insults personally. But, in fact, the insults that come our way have nothing to do with us and everything to do with the person or people doing the insulting (since, really, there is never any need to insult anyone). By shifting our focus away from ourselves, we can see insults more clearly for the markers of pathology that they are, and maybe even begin to feel for our insulter.

In Chapter 9, *How to party*, we examined how, in different times and places, people had ritualized ways of escaping from their artificial and restricted roles. But today, except maybe on the margins, we have lost the art of letting go, leading to a poverty or monotony of conscious experience and a loss of vital energy.

Finally, in Chapter 10, *How to think*, we found that what usually gets in the way of reason and reasoning is not stupidity as such, or feeble-mindedness, but fear and the thing that fear protects, namely, our self-esteem, our sense of self, our ego.

There are many ways to frame the Secret to Everything.

Here is one: Today, we are all busy trying to find ourselves, and it's almost impossible to shake off that mentality; but, actually, the more we forget about ourselves, the more we bury ourselves, the better we do.

Here's another, more radical formulation: The ego is an illusion, and this illusion is often unhelpful.

We came very close to this wisdom towards the end of Chapter 10, for example, when I quoted from the *Bhagavad Gita*:

> There has never been a time when you and I have not existed, nor will there be a time when we will cease to exist ... the wise are not deluded by these changes.

At that point, I had just finished coursing through a number of important ego defences. But one ego defence that remains to be discussed is reification [Latin, 'to make into a thing'], which involves turning an abstract and challenging notion into something more concrete and manageable.

The most common form of reification is anthropomorphization [Greek, 'to make into a man'], which involves turning a difficult idea into a human or humanoid figure, for example, death into the Grim Reaper, Lord Voldemort, or the Night King.

The ultimate anthropomorphization—of fate, of the universe, of all that is beyond our ability to comprehend—is the popular, almost cartoonish, image of God as an old man with a bushy beard and flowing robes, a kind of Aristotle with angels.

As with every other ego defence, the purpose of reification is, ultimately, to create and maintain a sense of the self as separate and special.

There is, therefore, an important sense in which the reifying self is itself reified.

~

But, really, what is the difference between you and me? What makes me me and you you?

Let's engage in a little thought experiment.

Imagine that you suffer an accident that leaves you lying brain-dead on a hospital bed. Your body is still alive, but you are no longer self-conscious, nor ever can be.

In these circumstances, are you still you?

Some thinkers have argued that a person at a time A is the same as a person at a time B because her body or brain is the same body or brain at both times, in the sense that they are continuous in space and time.

Others have argued that this is not the case: Instead, a person at a time A is the same as a person at a time B because they are psychologically continuous, that is, the mental states of the person at a time B derive or descend from the mental states of the person at a time A.

To help elucidate this problem, the philosopher Sydney Shoemaker asks us to imagine that science has advanced to such an extent that brain transplants are now possible.

Two men, Brown and Robinson, have their brains excised and exchanged. One of these two men dies on the operating table, but the other, say, the one with Brown's brain and Robinson's body (let us call him 'Brownson') pulls through and regains consciousness.

Who is this man Brownson, with Brown's brain and Robinson's body?

Although Brownson looks like Robinson, when asked his name, he replies 'Brown'. He does not recognize Robinson's wife, but welcomes Brown's wife and family as his own, and is privy to all of Brown's most intimate memories.

Most people would argue that Brownson is Brown, or, at least, much more Brown than Robinson—suggesting that a person is not reducible to his or her body.

This leaves us with just two possibilities: either Brownson is Brown because he has Brown's brain, or he is Brown because he is psychologically continuous with Brown.

Many people have survived with one half of their brain destroyed or surgically removed. So let's imagine that Brownson's brain (or, for that matter, anyone's brain, let's say, Wilson's) is now divided into two equal halves, and that each half is transplanted into a brainless body.

Following this Frankenstein procedure, two people awake who are both psychologically continuous with Wilson, and who have the same personality and memories as Wilson.

If they are both psychologically continuous with Wilson, are they both Wilson?

Most people would argue that, although they are very similar to each other, they are in fact two different people and, over time, will become increasingly different—much as one sibling from a pair of identical twins might grow up to become an accountant and the other a concert pianist.

In other words, it seems that what makes you a person depends causally upon the existence of your brain, but at the same time amounts to something more than just your brain.

What this might be is unclear, and perhaps for a reason.

We tend to think of our personhood as something concrete and tangible, something that exists 'out there' in the physical world and extends through space and time.

But it is possible that personhood is in fact nothing more than a product of our minds, a convenient concept or schema that enables us to relate our present self with our past, future, and conditional selves, and create an illusion of coherence and continuity from a succession of disparate perceptions, sensations, thoughts, feelings, and actions.

~

The idea that the ego is an illusion is probably most closely associated with the Buddha and Buddhism.

At the heart of Buddhism is the concept of the *anattā* or 'not-self', which is composed of five *skandhas* or elements, namely, body, sensation, perception, will, and consciousness. These five elements are in a constant state of flux but together create for the not-self the illusion of integrity and continuity, that is, the illusion of the self.

This explains why, when you try to become aware of your self, you can only ever become aware of such and such perception, such and such sensation, or such and such thought, but never of an actual, core self.

In Buddhist thought, the death of the empirical or bodily self leads to the disaggregation of the elements and to their re-aggregation into another not-self which is neither identical to nor entirely different from the previous not-self, but that forms part of a causal continuum with it. An analogy that is often used to describe this process of rebirth, or *samsāra*, is that of a flame passing from one candle to the next.

The cycle of rebirth can only be broken if the empirical, changing self is able to transcend its subjective and distorted image of the world, which is built around the 'I am' conceit. This, then, is heaven or *nirvana*. Nirvana, as I see it, rests on the understanding that consciousness is a sequence of conscious moments rather than the continuous, unbroken consciousness of the 'I am' conceit.

It is striking that the empiricist philosopher David Hume appeared to share in the Buddhist outlook:

> When I enter most intimately into what I call myself, I always stumble on some particular perception or other, of heat or cold, light or shade, love or hatred, pain or pleasure. I can never catch myself at any time without a perception, and never can observe anything but the perception. When my

> perceptions are removed for any time, as by sound sleep, so long am I insensible to myself, and may truly be said not to exist.

Our ego defences as broadly conceived—that is, not only our ego defences proper but also our moral codes, bourgeois values, habits, customs, culture, and other ties—may provide us with an illusion of self, but they also define us as such and such, and, in so doing, constrain our range of thought, feeling, and action.

Paradoxically, the very elements that furnish us with our sense of self are also those that prevent us from fulfilling our true promise and potential as human beings.

The Buddha taught that the failure to recognize the illusion of the self is the source of all ignorance and unhappiness. It is only by renouncing the self, that is, by dropping her ego defences and committing symbolic suicide, that a person is able to open up to different modes of being and relating and transform herself into a pure essence of humanity. In so doing, she becomes free to recast herself as a much more mindful, joyful, and productive person, and attains the only species of transcendence and immortality that is open to us, mere mortals.

And so, if we are to live, we must first learn to die.

The myth of Narcissus

The opposite of ego dissolution is narcissism, so let's re-examine these same notions through the prism of the Myth of Narcissus.

I've long been fascinated by this myth and its meaning—and I think I may finally have cracked it.

First, let's remind ourselves of the myth. In Ovid's version, the nymph Echo falls in love with Narcissus, a youth of extraordinary beauty. As a child, Narcissus had been prophesied by Teiresias, the blind prophet of Thebes, to 'live to a ripe old age, as long as he never knows himself'.

One day, Echo followed Narcissus through the woods as he hunted for stags. She longed to speak to him but dared not utter the first word. Overhearing her footsteps, the youth cried out, 'Who's there?' to which she responded, 'Who's there?' When at last she revealed herself, she leapt to embrace Narcissus, but he scorned her and cast her off. Echo spent the rest of her days pining for Narcissus, and slowly withered away until there was nothing left of her but her voice.

Some time after his encounter with Echo, Narcissus went to quench his thirst at a pool of water. Seeing his own image in the water, he fell in love with it. But each time he bent down to kiss it, it seemed to disappear. Narcissus grew thirstier and thirstier but would not leave or disturb the pool of water for fear of losing sight of his fine features. In the end, he died of thirst, and there, on that very spot, appeared the narcissus flower, with its bright face and bowed neck.

Figure 7: The narcissus flower, or daffodil.

What could this myth mean? On one level, it is an admonition to treat others as we would ourselves be treated—and in particular to be considerate in responding to the affections of others, which, as with Echo, are often so raw and visceral as to be existential. After being rejected by him, poor Echo had no self and no being outside of Narcissus, and 'slowly withered away until there was nothing left of her but her voice'.

On another level, the myth is a warning against vanity and self-love. Sometimes we get so caught up in ourselves, in our egos, that we lose sight of the bigger picture and, as a result, pass over the beauty and bounty that is life. Paradoxically, by being too wrapped up in ourselves, we actually restrict our range of perception and action and, ultimately, our potential as human beings. And so, in some sense, we kill ourselves, like so many ambitious or self-centred people. Treating other people badly, as Narcissus did, is a sure sign that we are still trapped in ourselves.

Teiresias prophesied that Narcissus would 'live to a ripe old age, as long as he never knows himself', because to truly know oneself is also to know that there is nothing to know. Our self, our ego, is nothing but an illusion, nothing more substantial than the unstable reflection that Narcissus tried in vain to kiss. Ultimately, Narcissus's ego boundaries dissolved in death, and he merged back into creation in the form of a flower.

Echo had not enough ego, and Narcissus far too much. The key is to find the right and dynamic equilibrium, to be secure in oneself and yet to be able to dissociate from the envelope that we happen to have been born into.

In Greek myth, the hero—Æneas, Heracles, Odysseus, Orpheus, Theseus—has to die and travel through the underworld before re-emerging as a hero.

He has to conquer himself, to die to himself, to become more than merely human.

For nothing is harder than to come back from hell.

THE ATARAXIA SERIES

> The happiness of your life depends upon the quality of your thoughts.
>
> — MARCUS AURELIUS, ROMAN EMPEROR AND STOIC PHILOSOPHER

In my work as a psychiatrist, I help to treat mental disorder—and, I'm delighted to say, most of the people I see do get better.

But why stop here?

I believe that there is much more to mental health than the mere absence of mental disorder.

Mental health is not just about surviving, but about thriving, about developing and expressing our highest, fullest potential as human beings.

Before Christianity, there were, of course, the pagan gods, Zeus and Jupiter and their ilk. But, especially for the high-minded, there were also a number of philosophical schools, the major ones being cynicism, stoicism, skepticism, and epicureanism.

Although each with its own outlook and method, all four schools aimed at the attainment of mental tranquillity and mastery, or *ataraxia*—making them, in my view, much more similar than different.

Ataraxia [Greek, 'lack of disturbance or trouble'] is also the guiding principle of this series, with each book, like each philosophy, adopting a distinct but complementary approach to peace of mind: exploring the deep origins of our distress in *The Meaning of Madness*; guarding against the demons of self-deception in *Hide and Seek*; refining our emotions in *Heaven and Hell*; regulating our relations with others in *For Better For Worse*; and, finally, honing our thinking skills in *Hypersanity*.

To recap, the five books in the series are:

1. The Meaning of Madness
2. Hide and Seek: The Psychology of Self-Deception
3. Heaven and Hell: The Psychology of the Emotions
4. For Better For Worse: Essays on Sex, Love, Marriage, and More
5. Hypersanity: Thinking Beyond Thinking

Although the series is numbered, each book can happily stand on its own—meaning that you can read just one or all five, and in whichever order you like.

Ataraxia is closely linked with eudaimonia, which is often translated as 'happiness' but which is, in fact, a much deeper, fuller, and richer concept, sometimes articulated in terms of flourishing, or living a life that is worthwhile and fulfilling.

The stakes could not be higher.

>>> Read Book 1 of the Ataraxia series

Printed in Great Britain
by Amazon

47230072R00076